The Caravan Goes On
How Aramco and Saudi Arabia Grew Up Together

Published by
Medina Publishing Ltd
310 Ewell Road
Surbiton
Surrey KT6 7AL
UK
medinapublishing.com

ISBN: 978-1-909339-18-7

Designed by Kitty Carruthers
Printed and bound by Toppan Leefung Printers Ltd, China

CIP Data: A catalogue record for this book is available from the British Library.

The Caravan Goes On

How Aramco and Saudi Arabia Grew Up Together

Frank Jungers

Medina Publishing

Acknowledgments

Saudi Aramco was most helpful in providing me information and assistance for this book, which contains a series of incidents and memories from my years in the Kingdom, my second home. The acknowledgments below therefore contain primarily both Saudi and American Aramcons. I am very fortunate to have been able to draw on their knowledge, memories and suggestions.

Robert Lebling, for final editing and guidance on readability and style; Khalid Al-Falih, President and CEO, Saudi Aramco, for encouragement and helpful assistance; Abdallah Jum'ah, former President and CEO, Saudi Aramco, for valuable, long experience and recall of Aramco's impact on the Saudi public and government; Haitham Al-Jehairan, for contact and coordination of input from Saudi Arabia; Nasser Al-Ajmi, former Senior Vice President, Saudi Aramco; Abdul Aziz Al-Khayyal, Senior Vice President, Saudi Aramco; the late Abdullah Naim, Vice President of Exploration; Mohammed Tahlawi, gatekeeper of facts and accuracy; Khalid Afandi, Aramco archival resources; Kyle Pakka, Aramco history contact; Arthur Clark, Aramco publications expert and valuable contact with Aramco annuitants; Peter Harrigan, active writer on Middle East historical subjects; Ali Baluchi, "Memory trigger" of the Aramco family and custodian of anecdotes; Susan Petrie, my executive assistant.

Of course, my wife Julie accompanied me on numerous trips to the Middle East. She patiently participated in discussions in Saudi Arabia, where her notes and recollections were always helpful. Saudi Aramco generously provided us with the opportunity to revisit parts of the country that I had not seen for many years, usually reviving old memories.

Photographic credits

Special thanks are owed to the Photo Unit of Saudi Aramco's Media Production Division for suggesting and providing numerous photographs.

We extend our sincere thanks to those Aramco photographers, both professional and amateur, now retired, whose pictures have been used in the book, including: Shaikh Amin, Wendy Cocker, Dorothy Miller and Bert Seal. Thanks also go to independent photographer Isabel "Didi" Cutler.

Contents

The spectacular dune formations in the Rubʿ al-Khali, or Empty Quarter, as seen from the air.

Prologue

Due partly to the forces of history and partly to the fortuitous discovery of oil, a peninsula vaguely identified as "Arabia" on still-incomplete world maps began to receive world attention in the early years of the 20th century.

After World War I, in the wake of the collapse of the Ottoman Empire, the British and French worked to establish and expand their spheres of influence in the Arabic-speaking lands of the Middle East, particularly in areas perceived to have strategic or economic value. These areas extended mainly from Mesopotamia (now Iraq) to the Levant and Egypt. The Arabian Peninsula – close to the action but not central to it – was to some extent "watched over" by the British from their outposts along its southern and eastern edges (now the countries of Bahrain, Oman, Yemen and the United Arab Emirates) as well as from faraway India.

The Turks, rulers of the Ottoman Empire, had made sporadic efforts – occasionally hindered by the British – to establish control over the Red Sea coast southward as far as the Islamic holy cities of Mecca and Medina. But neither the Ottomans nor the British made specific land claims in Arabia. Although there were Ottoman forts in eastern Arabia, there was no defined colonial power controlling the many cities, towns, villages and tribes spread across this huge peninsula. Apart from some inconclusive oil exploration by the British in the Farasan Islands off Arabia's Red Sea coast in 1912, no specific exploration had been carried out in Arabia to discover oil or other valuable natural resources.

A nation began to coalesce as Abdulaziz Al Saud, leader of the Saud clan, consolidated control in the central Najd region, with Riyadh as his center of operations and later as his capital. This nation-building process began in 1902 with the capture of Riyadh and progressed slowly and by steps, eventually encompassing all of the territory that we now call Saudi Arabia. It involved uniting a scattered yet socially cohesive population of tribal families and isolated cities, towns and villages across the peninsula.

The charismatic King Abdulaziz Al Saud (better known in the West as Ibn Saud) proved to be a wise and persuasive leader, establishing the Kingdom of Saudi Arabia in 1932. The financial needs of the new government and country were increasing and becoming critical at this time, during the Great Depression. Few natural resources had

Left: King Abdulaziz Al Saud greets visitors at Khazem Palace in Jeddah in 1946

Opposite: Karl Twitchell's motorized "caravan" stops at a major watering hole on the western side of the Dahna desert in the Hejaz in 1932.

been identified in this embryonic nation, which was larger than the combined area of France, Germany, Italy, Spain and Britain – or equal to the land area of the United States east of the Mississippi River – and which lacked a national communications grid and modern transportation system.

The British made several attempts to obtain oil concessions in Saudi Arabia through high-level discussions with Finance Minister Sheikh Abdullah Sulaiman, but none of these discussions were substantive. In fact, King Abdulaziz believed that the British were not serious about the country's oil prospects, since they did not make any significant cash offers in these talks.

In February 1933 the Standard Oil Company of California (Socal), today known as Chevron, which had a presence in Bahrain and was interested in securing an oil concession in Saudi Arabia, sent mining engineer Karl Twitchell and lawyer and land-lease expert Lloyd Hamilton to Jeddah, the Kingdom's commercial and, at the time, diplomatic capital. Twitchell and Hamilton brought their wives along with them. The Saudis were impressed with their seriousness and were interested in making a deal, so negotiations began in earnest. The Americans received unexpected support

from a British advisor to King Abdulaziz, Harry St John (Abdullah) Philby, who had no sympathy for Britain's commercial interests in Saudi Arabia. Philby was a noted Arabist, explorer and writer. Born in Ceylon (later Sri Lanka), he had worked for British intelligence in Baghdad and in British-Mandate Palestine. Afterwards, he converted to Islam and became a close advisor of King Abdulaziz.

The proposed Concession Agreement was presented to the King's council for approval in May 1933. King Abdulaziz – who reportedly sat quietly, almost as if dozing, through the reading of the specific terms of the contract – became suddenly alert when the droning voice of the reader ceased, having completed all 37 separate articles. At this point, the King said: "Put your trust in God and sign." His Finance Minister, Abdullah Sulaiman, did so. Sulaiman had been advised by Sir Andrew Ryan, the first British Minister to Saudi Arabia, to accept the American offer because "it was most unlikely that there was oil there anyway."[1] Ryan himself had for a time led the British negotiations with the Saudis on behalf of the Iraq Petroleum Company (IPC), but the British had been unwilling to come anywhere near the Saudi position and eventually bowed out.

The terms of the Concession Agreement were considered "stiff" by the international oil industry. The accord provided the Kingdom up-front with certain sums of badly-needed cash in pounds sterling, gold or its equivalent – an initial loan of £30,000 and after 18 months another £20,000, plus annual rent of £5,000, not including oil royalties and certain other payments – amounts that after 80 years of inflation seem very small indeed. The original agreement also provided that Socal would pay the Saudi Government £50,000 upon discovery of oil in commercial quantities, plus £50,000 a year later – both sums advances against future royalties.

The far-reaching Concession Agreement was carefully and faithfully followed and honored by both sides in the decades to come. The agreement covered 320,000 square miles (829,000 square kilometers) of Saudi territory, along with preferential rights to bid for additional land. Socal formed a subsidiary called the California Arabian Standard Oil Company (CASOC) to administer the concession. In 1939 – following discovery of crude oil in commercial quantities the previous year near the company's camp, which is today the oil city of Dhahran – CASOC negotiated a supplemental

---

[1] Sander, Nestor. *Ibn Saud: King by Conquest*. Tucson, Ariz.: Hats Off Books, 2001.

agreement that increased the total area of the deal to 425,000 square miles (1.1 million square kilometers). The deal included additional cash for the Kingdom and other important provisions, such as the requirement to build a refinery to provide the country with refined petroleum products (a provision featured in the original agreement as well) and subsequent relinquishment of acreage over set periods of time to ensure expeditious exploration over the years.

During the years between signature of the concession in 1933 and the discovery of oil in 1938, CASOC expanded geological exploration and began operations that focused first on providing services for American geologists in the field. Initial geological crews began arriving in 1933. CASOC's activities took on a new permanence with the arrival of the first few wives and families of American employees in Dhahran in April 1937. Expanded operations meant serious attention had to be paid to providing support, such as food imports, motor vehicles, machinery, repair facilities, housing and various kinds of amenities such as one might find in a small American town – but with added complexities in view of the fact that the residential camp was located in a harsh desert climate far from outside support.

During this pioneering stage, I was spending my childhood years – up to age 13 – in the farmlands of North Dakota, followed by eight more years in Oregon and Washington, where I attended high school and college. I had little or no idea that I would eventually be leaving home to live and work in a distant and – to me, at least – exotic land.

In eastern Saudi Arabia, Bedouin guides and local villagers were being hired in small numbers as laborers, drivers, mechanics and helpers. They required training, living accommodations and basic amenities. Initially, the number of Saudis employed was small, but jobs were highly prized and eagerly sought after by local residents. Thus the CASOC community and its needs grew steadily.

After oil was discovered in 1938, the oil company began to hire personnel to operate new facilities required to produce, process and transport the petroleum. The Government began to think about using its new-found wealth to enhance the lives of the people. The company's growth slowed to a standstill during World War II, after which operations restarted in earnest, as both Saudi Arabia and the company that in 1944 became the Arabian American Oil Company (Aramco) began a long and steady period of development. Both entities needed to deal with a welter of multicultural workforce challenges. Many of these came about because Americans and Saudis had hardly heard of each other prior to being required to work and live together. It remains one of the most remarkable and fortunate aspects of the story that "Aramcons" developed into a close-knit community and the company and the Government expanded in parallel, relying on each other to achieve common goals. Both the company and the country were confronting new challenges – entering a brave new world, as it were – and they worked in partnership to achieve their respective and common goals.

I became a member of the unique Aramco community in 1947, and played my own small part in the development of what became the world's largest energy enterprise in a country that contains the primary holy places of a major world religion – Islam – and sits astride hundreds of billions of barrels of crude oil, the largest known proven reserves on the planet.[2]

The Kingdom of Saudi Arabia and the company that became Aramco were roughly the same age, and were destined to grow up together. In the process, over decades, both underwent dramatic transformations.

This is my version of the Aramco story. It is my sincere hope that it will add some insights and new perspectives to one of the most unique and important relationships of modern times.

Frank Jungers

---

[2] Saudi Arabia has roughly 260 billion barrels of proven reserves. Yes, the word "proven" is important. Oil reserves come in three categories: possible, probable and proven. The first two categories are considered "unproven." Possible reserves generally claim a 10 percent certainty of recovery, and probable reserves a 50 percent level. Proven reserves are delineated by wells and have a 90 percent or higher certainty of recovery, given existing conditions and technology.

Introduction

The history of oil in the Middle East speaks of the profound effects this precious natural resource and commodity has had on the economic and political systems of the world.[1] The Arabian American Oil Company (Aramco), a major part of this history, grew from a tiny American-owned operation in the deserts of Saudi Arabia in the 1930s into the world's largest oil-producing company, Saudi Aramco, now owned by the Saudi Government and operated by Saudi nationals. More importantly, the company became a key factor in the lives of many Middle Eastern Arabs, especially those who lived in Saudi Arabia and neighboring countries along the western side of the Arabian Gulf.

Numerous books have been written on this broad topic, most covering oil, politics and the economics of the time and the region. But few have focused on the impact that the Aramco enterprise had on the people of the region. The American oil adventure

---

[1] This introduction was partially taken from an Oral History developed by the University of California at Berkeley's Bancroft Library, for which I wrote the original introduction.

in Saudi Arabia began in 1933 and lasted until 1988, when Aramco was transformed into Saudi Aramco. The American oil companies that formed Aramco remain major customers of its Saudi-owned successor company, and American professionals continue to contribute expertise to this enterprise, now operated by Saudi

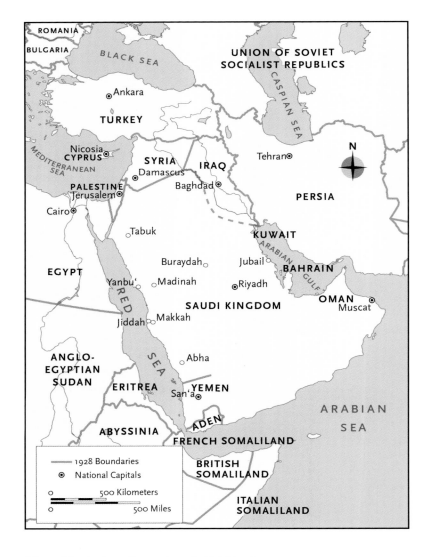

Map of the Arabian Peninsula with 1928 borders.

executives who rose through the company's ranks as Saudi Aramcons. In a period of 75-plus years, from the 1930s to today, the people of Saudi Arabia in particular have been confronted with tremendous changes that have challenged their culture and altered their lifestyle and aspirations. It is indeed a tribute to the remarkable people of Saudi Arabia and other Gulf states that they could assimilate the impacts of industrialization – indeed globalization – and the presence of foreign cultures in their midst without experiencing the deep resentment or even rebellion that occurred in developing countries where such social and cultural contrasts were even less pronounced.

Many factors played a role in this remarkably "peaceful" development process, but at the forefront were the policies of Aramco, which were based on the principle that the company should behave as a good citizen of the country in which it operated. That this would be the company's mode of operation was a far-reaching decision, consciously taken.

The resulting values that Saudis and Americans shared over the years shaped a record marked, by and large, by cooperation and mutual respect on both the individual level and that of company–government relations. This was in sharp contrast to elsewhere in the world, where foreign-owned oil companies often had adversarial, exploitative or even colonialist relationships with their host governments.

Aramco, however, implemented a special set of well-thought-out policies, including: using the best available technologies; maximizing training and the development of Saudi manpower; encouraging the creation and participation of local businesses and other enterprises in its activities; and respectfully observing Saudi law and customs.

The Saudi Government and, in turn, Saudi citizens themselves would from time to time tweak or sidestep certain rules and customs to accommodate the Americans and the needs of industry. These measures were in the Kingdom's self-interest, as well as in those of the company. But this unique course was driven by more than commercial self-interest: from many other perspectives – global, regional, domestic – it was the right thing to do. A symbolic but significant early indication of the enterprise's awareness of national sensitivities was changing the name of the business in 1944 from California Arabian Standard Oil Company to Arabian American Oil Company – with "Arabian" ahead of "American" in the new title. Of similar importance was the decision, in the mid-1950s, to transfer the company's headquarters from New York, N.Y., to Dhahran, the locus of company activities on Saudi Arabia's Gulf coast.

These policies and Aramco's insistence on excellence in its operations created a feeling of value and camaraderie among all employees, especially Saudis and Americans. By the mid-1950s, capable Saudis began to appear in supervisory positions in ever-increasing numbers. They in turn had many American and other foreign technicians and specialists working for them. The development of Saudi employees – mandated in general terms in the 1933 Concession Agreement that launched the exploration for oil in Saudi Arabia – was the result of training and personal achievement, and tended to accelerate the training effort and subsequent Saudi promotions. This "Saudization" strategy culminated in the eventual promotion of a Saudi geologist, Ali I. Al-Naimi, to the position of Aramco president and chief executive officer.

After the Saudi Government purchased the company from its American shareholders, it was renamed "Saudi Aramco" in 1988.[2] The choice of that working name recognized not only the value of the Aramco brand throughout the Middle East and around the world, but also the goodwill created by the company in the Kingdom. In nearly all other oil-producing countries, foreign-owned oil companies

King Abdullah, center, is escorted by Petroleum Minister Ali Al-Naimi, second from right, and Saudi Aramco President and CEO Abdallah Jum'ah, second from left, at a ceremonial event.

---

[2] Its formal name is the Saudi Arabian Oil Company (Saudi Aramco).

were nationalized and government-managed, i.e., government employees were installed in company management positions. In the case of Saudi Aramco, the existing company management – most of whom were already Saudis – remained in place, with the Minister of Petroleum and Mineral Resources taking the position of Chairman of the Board of Directors. At the time of writing, the Minister himself is indeed a former Aramcon – Ali Al-Naimi

Throughout its development, Aramco published no official company histories,[3] but the memories of Saudi and expatriate employees, myself included, are a rich source of fact, anecdote and opinion that illuminate the history of Aramco and of Saudi Arabia. Some of the incidents are humorous and even somewhat amazing when viewed through modern eyes – collectively, they provide a unique perspective on an era that spans much of the "Petroleum Century," highlighted by the parallel creation and growth of both a company and a country. Unfortunately, the number of ex-Aramcons from this era is dwindling, and with their passing much knowledge and Aramco lore is disappearing. This existence of ours is indeed fragile and short-lived.

With this in mind, I have recorded some of my memories, particularly through the use of anecdotes and by briefly describing Aramco for young men and women unaware of how and why today's Saudi Aramco came to be.

Ali Al-Niami at work in Aramco operating facilities after college graduation pictured with Aramco photographer Shaikh Amin.

---

[3] Aramco did publish successive handbooks to familiarize new employees and others with the company's history and Middle Eastern context. As Saudi Aramco, in 2011, the company published its first official company history, *Energy to the World: The Story of Saudi Aramco.*

This book, then, is not my autobiography, nor does it cover my life and times during my 30 years with Aramco (from 1947 to 1978), most of which were spent living and working in Saudi Arabia. This was a marvelous career during which I received a memorable and broad education and was given the opportunity to use it by helping to create a unique bicultural legacy – what I call the Aramco Legacy.

With the help of Aramco and its past publications and records I have attempted to describe the Aramco Legacy, and how it came into existence as the Kingdom and the company matured together. Where applicable, I have also referenced other books written about Saudi Arabia, its geography, its oil and gas, and its own unique leadership. This book is not meant to be a history of Aramco, nor one of Saudi Arabia, or oil, or negotiations, or legal landmarks. Rather, I hope that these memories, anecdotes and facts will serve as worthwhile "brush strokes" in a painting that will become more and more complete as other Aramcons and scholars contribute to it, adding their own colors and designs.

An exploration field crew moves through the desert between Hofuf and Yabrin, southwest of Dhahran, 1939-40.

Chapter 1
Aramco's Origins

The American oil industry played a unique role in the early development of modern Saudi Arabia. Aramco was the instrument that made so much possible. What began as a new company's search for a precious energy resource in time evolved into a much broader effort that supported the young Kingdom's development goals. The oil company became a valuable instrument in the Saudi Government's tool chest of available options for quickly providing infrastructure and services that would help build a modern nation. Consequently, as the company grew, so did the new nation.

The first American participant in this adventure was Standard Oil Company of California (Socal), today called Chevron. Eventually three other U.S. oil majors joined the effort.

In 1933, after Saudi Arabia granted an oil concession to Socal, the company formed the California Arabian Oil Company (CASOC), a Delaware-registered

A red tractor trailer follows bulldozers in the dunes of the Saudi desert. Photo by Bert Seal.

subsidiary, to hold all of the Saudi Arabian assets and administer the concession. CASOC eventually became the company called Aramco.

Socal had another affiliate in the Arabian Gulf region, the Bahrain Petroleum Company Ltd (Bapco). For political and legal reasons and because Bapco was British-controlled, Socal opted to keep a clear separation between the two concessions.[1] However, Bapco's facilities on nearby Bahrain, a group of islands about 15 miles (24 km.) off the Saudi coast, were used temporarily by CASOC geologists for communications, freight and part-time living quarters until infrastructure could be developed on the mainland. Initially, large freight items such as cars and construction materials were shipped to Bahrain and then brought to Saudi Arabia on traditional wooden sailing vessels called dhows. It did not take long to discover that cars were often

---

[1] Bapco was technically a subsidiary of Socal, but it was registered in the British Commonwealth (in Canada) and the company's leadership was British.

useless in the sands of Arabia – at least until bigger and wider tires were developed. Instead, camels (with their broad footpads) were much more capable of traversing shifting, hilly sand-dune terrain. Saudi merchants gladly furnished camels for those early geologists and their gear. It wasn't long before cars with better tires began arriving in Saudi Arabia, and the geologists quickly switched to motorized transportation.

Socal's first notion that there might be oil in the Arabian Peninsula arose when Bapco geologists discovered a small oilfield under a rocky hill outcrop on Bahrain.[2] On a clear day, while standing on that hill and gazing west across the Gulf waters to the Saudi coast, geologists saw similar outcropping hills on the horizon (known locally as Jabal Umm Er Rus, around which Dhahran was later built). Fred Davies, the geologist later assigned to lead the CASOC operation (and who subsequently became CEO of Aramco in the 1950s), was one of the chief advocates for securing a concession in Arabia. He insisted that the geologic structure they were viewing on the mainland was similar to Bapco's in Bahrain and argued that the vastly bigger area of Saudi Arabia was likely to contain bigger oil reservoirs. The Saudis turned down initial requests for permission to explore the mainland. But by 1933 Socal had secured an oil concession, and geologists began scouring eastern Saudi Arabia for telltale signs of petroleum and drilling exploration wells.

By 1936, only minor oil shows had been identified, and Socal was encountering considerable, ongoing costs in the Kingdom. In Bahrain, meanwhile, Socal's affiliate Bapco was looking for better markets in the East to which it could sell its production. Another American oil major, the Texas Company (or Texaco), had already developed a number of markets in Asia and was seeking ways to meet its customers' demand for increased production. Negotiations between Socal and Texaco led to the creation of a jointly-held marketing company called Caltex (the California Texas Oil Company), which would provide an Asian outlet for Bapco crude. At the same time, in September 1936 Texaco acquired 50 percent of CASOC for cash – enough funds

---

[2] The earliest attempt to exploit the mineral resources of mainland Arabia came about a decade earlier, in 1923, when Abdulaziz granted a modest oil concession to Major Frank Holmes of New Zealand. Holmes represented a London financial syndicate; the group failed to interest any oil companies in the concession, which soon lapsed. In 1931–32, Vermont mining engineer Karl Twitchell criss-crossed Arabia at the request of the Saudi ruler, seeking out water sources, oil seeps and mineral outcrops. Twitchell was soon retained by Socal to pursue a concession agreement.

to allow for continued exploration and drilling operations in Saudi Arabia. CASOC thus remained the operating company for two shareholders in the Kingdom, Socal and Texaco.

As it turned out, the rocky outcrops spotted from Bahrain were part of a single structure – now known as the Dammam Dome – overlying substantial reserves of crude oil and non-associated natural gas.[3] A major oil reservoir was finally discovered in March 1938 in a deep zone penetrated by Dammam Well No. 7. Five years of dogged tenacity and hard work finally paid off.

The first exploration wells drilled into the Dammam Dome had proven to be dry holes – or practically so. Rumors spread that officials back at company headquarters in San Francisco were beginning to have doubts about the Saudi concession. CASOC chief geologist Max Steineke is credited with persuading Socal to continue drilling deeper into the dome, where his study of the geology of the peninsula convinced him that there was producible oil. Drillers eventually hit what is known as the Arab Formation – the principal oil reservoir of what geologists call the Upper Jurassic sequence in the Middle East, which we now know holds about half the known oil and gas resources of the entire world. One level of this formation, the Arab D, also provides the oil of the gargantuan Ghawar Field, southwest of Dammam. Ghawar, discovered in 1948 and still a top producer, is the largest oil field in the world.

Today Saudis call Dammam Well No. 7 the "Prosperity Well." It was so named by the current Saudi King, Abdullah, when he was Crown Prince, to honor its role in helping to initiate the Kingdom's march to economic development. The historic well has been capped and now serves as an important monument, visited by those interested in the early days of oil in Saudi Arabia.

Well No. 7 produced crude oil at high rates, requiring immediate construction of the Kingdom's first refining plant and shipping terminals. The first oil tanker, the *D.G. Scofield,* a Socal vessel, loaded on May 1, 1939, at the Ras Tanura terminal, north of Dhahran. It was a banner day for the young Kingdom. King Abdulaziz and a large retinue traveled from Riyadh and Jeddah for his first visit to the company. In

---

[3] In addition to the gas dissolved in oil (called associated gas), in 1957 Aramco made the first discovery of non-associated gas in a deeper formation. Subsequently, enormous reserves of non-associated gas were discovered in Qatar, Iran and Abu Dhabi.

a ceremony at Ras Tanura, the King turned the valve that began the historic loading of the tanker.

Unfortunately, the beginning of World War II cut short the company's growth, causing it to virtually shut in operations until 1944.

On January 31, 1944, CASOC and its two shareholders changed the name of the company to the Arabian American Oil Company. They took this step primarily because the name CASOC implied there was only one shareholder and ignored the 50 percent interest of Texaco. It is worth noting that all parties agreed early on that the dual-country relationship should be designated in the new title and that Arabia should come first in the name of the company. Thus the acronym Aramco was born.

That same year, the company began stepping up its expenditure significantly, to produce, refine and ship oil to a world about to begin its recovery from a devastating global war. The two Aramco shareholders realized they needed greater marketing and financial resources to develop the potential of this costly, distant Arabian reservoir. These needs led to talks with additional oil majors. After intensive negotiations, agreement was reached January 31, 1946, to sell 40 percent of Aramco to two new partners – Jersey Standard Oil (later called Exxon) and Socony-Vacuum, later known as Mobil. (Over the years, shareholder names changed frequently. From here on, for clarity, we will use the current names of these two companies, Exxon and Mobil.) There were now four American shareholder owners in the venture, three with an equal 30 percent stake and the fourth, Mobil, with a minority 10 percent holding.

The partners agreed that despite Mobil's smaller share, all four owners would have equal representation on the Aramco board. The ownership inequality and directorship equality later came to present a major negotiating problem as Aramco entered a period of tremendous expansion. As the four companies' worldwide market shares changed, these fierce international competitors needed to buy Aramco oil in different percentages than indicated by their 30–30–30–10 percent ownership shares. At the same time, in the 1946 agreement to sell shares to Exxon and Mobil, all four parties agreed that their decisions regarding Aramco should be consistent with Aramco's overall best interests. This point proved most significant in the remarkable success and growth of this unique venture. For example, Mobil's 10 percent share was inadequate to satisfy its market growth. Thus Mobil had to negotiate with the other three shareholders to obtain more Aramco oil – but at what price?

Chapter 2
My Road to Aramco

I was born in July 1926 in Regent, a small town in Hettinger County in the southwest corner of North Dakota, a state that for the most part was divided up into large wheat and grain farms. Regent was about 50 miles south of the Badlands, an area that had gained fame as a favorite destination of America's 26th President, Theodore Roosevelt. He is considered by many to have been our country's first "Conservationist President," and it was in the Badlands that many of his personal interests and concerns about preserving local wildlife developed, giving rise to his later environmental efforts.

My father and his seven brothers worked on the large family farm and in the Regent general store. In addition to working on his farm, my grandfather was also the Regent postmaster, and he had a natural interest in stamps of all countries. As a small boy, I can remember him showing me how to keep a stamp album, and he often called me into the post office to give me stamps. People who received mail from abroad gave him permission to carefully remove the foreign stamps from the envelopes. By mounting them in my albums and reading about them, I received an effective early geography lesson that was to serve me well. I became interested in learning about foreign lands, and in time would find myself living overseas for a major portion of my life.

Along with his other grandsons, I worked on the farm in the harvesting season, and at age 11 my grandfather taught me to drive an old red Reo Speed Wagon to haul wheat from the threshing field to the grain elevator in town a few miles away. He paid me a dollar a day to drive the durable old truck. The classic truck was the early ancestor of the pickup truck, the essential oil industry vehicle that I was to become even more familiar with later in Arabia.[1]

However, in the mid-1930s, a vast, crippling drought struck the Great Plains of the central United States, causing devastating dust storms in a climatic event known as the "Dust Bowl" and adding insult to the injury of the ongoing Great Depression. As the farm fields dried out, locust-like grasshoppers appeared in cycles that actually darkened the skies like a biblical plague and destroyed the few wheat plants that had survived the drought. As one North Dakotan described it at the time: "This 1934 drought has had a devastating effect on the economic welfare of farmers, and therefore, the state itself. … The invasion of grasshopper hordes has made the situation even worse. They eat everything – even fence posts. The clouds of hoppers were so thick at Mott in Hettinger County that the city had to turn on its streetlights during the day. At Killdeer the grasshoppers lay in piles four inches thick on the streets, making the driving of a car almost impossible." [2]

I later experienced similar phenomena in Saudi Arabia. There, blinding sandstorms from the north called *shammals* swept across the Arabian Peninsula, mainly during the summer. And from time to time, mostly in seven-year cycles, huge swarms of

---

[1] The REO or Reo Speed Wagon was a rugged light truck manufactured by Ransom E. Olds' REO Motor Car Company from 1915 to 1953. A popular rock band of the 1970s and 1980s borrowed the name, pronouncing the first three letters individually rather than as a single word.

[2] Dr. D. Jerome Tweton, "If 1933 Was Bad, 1934 Was Really Bad: Drought Ravages State," *The North Star Dakotan*, December 31, 1934.

A sandstorm, or shamal, *strikes a neighborhood in Dhahran. Photo by Wendy Cocker.*

desert locusts arrived from East Africa, darkening the Arabian skies and causing devastation to precious grazing lands. The desert locust, traditionally a serious threat to agricultural production in the Middle East, in previous centuries was cooked and eaten by some Bedouins as a protein source. But today any locusts that reach Arabia from Africa are likely to be contaminated with pesticides and are no longer eaten. During the early 1960s, Aramco provided aviation and ground support for locust control teams in the Kingdom. The Eastern Province of Saudi Arabia has long been a battleground in frequent assaults against the desert locust, because that area served as a springboard for airborne locust invasions of the Indian subcontinent.

Like the Native Americans who have lived in America for some 11,000 years, the homesteaders who arrived from Europe in the late 19th century are acknowledged to have been just as tenacious, surviving the extreme climate and unforgiving conditions. I like to think that my prairie roots run deep, and that they have served me well and helped me appreciate both the harshness and beauty of Arabia.

Farming became so unprofitable during the prolonged drought that many farmers left the parched Dakota fields. My father moved west to Oregon and purchased a gasoline service station there in 1939. Then, at the age of 13, I drove the family car to Eugene, Oregon, where we settled.

I completed high school a year earlier than most others in my age group. Then I spent a year and a half in a U.S. Navy training program, at which point World War II ended and I was released from the Navy. I continued my studies at the University of Washington, receiving a Bachelor's degree in mechanical engineering (BSME) in August 1947. Even though I had worked in a number of part-time jobs during these years, like many new graduates I was in debt.

Prior to graduation in 1947, a recruiter from Aramco visited our campus along with other recruiting companies seeking to interview engineering graduates. I was fortunate to receive a number of job offers, and I chose Aramco, primarily because the salary was considerably higher than those of the other companies and I needed to repay my debts. I had almost no knowledge of the Middle East – bar the stamps! – but the job did sound like an interesting, pioneering effort. I was told I would be assigned to an engineering office in San Francisco and could expect to be reassigned to Saudi Arabia in a matter of months.

And so, on September 1, 1947, I set out on what was to become a remarkable overseas experience in a most unusual career. Only one other engineer at the University of Washington was offered a job with Aramco at that time: Harold T. "Hal" Fogelquist also accepted the offer and joined me in San Francisco.

Chapter 3
An Arabian Adventure

When I began my career with Aramco, the company's main office was next to Socal's headquarters in San Francisco. In September 1947, I was assigned to an engineering organization there, and I quickly set to work on a project that Bechtel Corporation was engineering and building to increase the capacity of Aramco's refinery at Ras Tanura. It was, for those times, a large project.

After we completed our work in San Francisco, the project was ready for implementation. All of the main equipment had been shipped and I was sent to Ras Tanura to assist in the construction of the project, serving as liaison between Aramco and Bechtel.

I left for Arabia from New York's Idlewild Airport (today's John F. Kennedy International Airport). My first flight was aboard a Douglas DC-4 – a four-engine aircraft that was unpressurized but was then the world's most modern long-range

Young Frank Jungers in an office at Aramco early in his career.

commercial aircraft. Flying to Saudi Arabia took two days, with an overnight stop in Portugal. Aramco owned and operated two such aircraft, the *Flying Camel* and the *Flying Gazelle*, which flew in opposite directions. I took the *Camel*. The *Gazelle* was in Saudi Arabia and would fly the return route.

These planes shuttled back and forth between the United States and Saudi Arabia. Because they were not pressurized, the flights were at low altitude, at times involving some rough riding, on a route that stretched from New York to Gander, Newfoundland, and then on to Portugal. There the crew and passengers rested for 24 hours before moving on. Everyone on my flight was housed in a coastal area outside Lisbon called Estoril, known for its famous gambling house, Casino Estoril, said to be the largest in Europe at the time and the inspiration for Ian Fleming's James Bond novel, Casino Royale. This was my first encounter with casinos. I didn't have much money, but I lost the lion's share of what I had, despite the efforts of some Portuguese to assist me! The plane flew on the next day, stopping to refuel in Damascus, Syria, before completing its final leg to Dhahran in Saudi Arabia.

In those days our company flights landed at Dhahran Airfield, built by the U.S. military near the end of World War II. In 1961, the airfield became Dhahran International Airport, serving airlines from around the world. Today, commercial airline traffic (and that of Saudi Aramco) flies into the sprawling King Fahd International Airport, west of Dammam. The old Dhahran airport has become a base for the Royal Saudi Air Force.

My assignment at Ras Tanura began shortly after the Christmas season. I sometimes did shift work, and during these shifts I became acquainted with the first Saudis I ever met. Most spoke little or no English, and I of course spoke no Arabic. It wasn't long before I enrolled in a company-sponsored course in basic Arabic, taught by a Palestinian instructor.

During the construction project, which lasted about three months, I worked on shifts with Bechtel contractors and with another Aramco employee who had a great deal of experience in inspection work. He checked on the quality of the work done by Bechtel. In addition to the Saudis working at the refinery, Aramco employed some Indians and Pakistanis, as well as some Italians who had been recruited from Eritrea in East Africa. These Italians, who worked mainly in the maintenance crews, were former civilian workers who had been left stranded in Eritrea by Mussolini when British forces defeated Italy in the East Africa campaign of 1941. Mussolini was disgraced by the defeat and was reluctant to allow these civilians back home, where they might tell the truth about what had happened. Aramco hired a number of these Italians, who were craftsmen or had other useful skills.

Many of the important processes in oil refineries involve the heating and partial evaporation of hydrocarbons using large furnaces. One of the major elements of the Ras Tanura project was welding an additional 50 feet of furnace stack or chimney on

The Ras Tanura beach, with the refinery tanks and the terminal control tower in the background. Photo by Wendy Cocker.

top of an existing stack that was already 100 feet high. This would give more air, or draft, to the furnaces below.

The piece of stack in question was raised between two gin poles and set on top of the existing stack prior to welding. The welding was all done by hand, primarily by American welders. By that time, a number of Saudi employees were in training as welders and assisted on the project, but were not yet qualified to make critical welds.

The welding took quite a while and involved a number of weld passes (or single progressions of welding along a joint). One night the Bechtel general foreman, whose name I recall was Hughie Dyer, announced to me that all welding had been completed up on the stack. The welders were waiting for permission to come down, and Hughie said they needed my approval.

I said: "Well, if you think the welds are good …"

He interrupted. "I think they are – but you're the representative and so you, as the representative, should go up there and check those welds."

Hughie was old enough to be my father – perhaps even older. I was a young kid, a raw, inexperienced engineer, and he was giving me a hard time. Everyone, American and Saudi alike, was listening keenly and waiting for my decision.

There was no way for me to back out. Much to my dismay, it wasn't long before I was riding a bosun's chair up the full 100 feet, at which level they had built a walk around the stack for the welders to work on, consisting of two six-inch boards on which they sat and welded. The big trick was to get out of the bosun's chair and onto these boards, where I was supposed to walk around the circumference of the stack and inspect the welds. The stack was huge and the wind was blowing. A few Saudi helpers got me off the bosun's chair and helped me move around the 30-foot-diameter stack. They had learned how to walk around upright on these two boards. There was no guardrail on the platform. I was terrified – there was no way I was going to stand up. So I crawled on my hands and knees. The Saudis urged me to stand up and walk, and one of the American welders chimed in, saying I really should walk it, but I was unable to comply.

I did finally make it around the stack, and they showed me how good the welds were. Eventually I got back into the bosun's chair and by the time I was safely on the ground, I leveled my anger at Hughie Dyer.

He said: "Well, what do you think?"

"Hughie," I said, "it's not good enough. You need *one more pass all the way around.*"

"You gotta be kidding," he said. He was stunned.

"No, I'm not kidding," I said. "Hughie, you need to make another pass."

He tried to talk me out of it, saying this meant unnecessary cost.

"Hughie," I said, "I don't care if I am fired for this, but you are going make another pass."

That was my first trial-by-fire as a supervisor!

The Saudi employees were surprised I had insisted on another welding pass, but a few of them understood what was happening and realized what this fellow had been trying to do to me. They winked at me in agreement – I suppose they didn't much like Hughie Dyer either.

When the Ras Tanura project was completed, I was sent back to the U.S. to wrap up final work on the project files – but I was also marking time, because there was no available company housing in Saudi Arabia for either bachelors or married employees, and I was newly married. The Italian employees were living in tents in a temporary camp near Ras Tanura – as yet they had no permanent buildings. The Saudis were housed in concrete-block buildings that had been erected very quickly without much attention to architectural detail. In the eyes of Saudi employees, more used to the openness of desert life, the buildings needed better ventilation in the extremely hot climate of eastern Saudi Arabia. These buildings became quite unpopular. The Americans had a camp of their own, but most lived in barracks, apart from a handful of houses built for families. Most American employees were waiting for family housing to be built so that they could bring their wives and children to the Kingdom. Housing was allocated on a priority basis, with some candidates waiting for more than six months.

In the late summer of 1948, I returned to Saudi Arabia on a permanent assignment as a project engineer at the Ras Tanura Refinery. Aramco had recently established a new requirement for employees assigned to the Kingdom – an orientation program at Riverhead, on Long Island, N.Y., where the company leased facilities that had been used as a military airport during World War II. There, Saudi instructors gave newly-hired employees and transferees a three-week general course in the basics of spoken Saudi Arabic and the customs of the Saudis and people elsewhere in the Middle East. We lived with these Saudis, so they learned something about our culture as well. We all came away from the experience with a basic knowledge of each other.

One of my Saudi instructors was Mohammed A. Salamah, two of whose sons later went on to pursue successful careers with the company. Mohammed was an enterprising young man and a good teacher. In his spare time, he headed into the town of Riverhead and took boxing lessons at a local gym. He developed a reputation as a pretty good boxer. I believe that when he returned to the Kingdom he gave up the sport, but we always kidded him about that early experience. Other Saudi instructors whose names I recall include Khalifah Al-Dowsari, 'Abd al-Rahman Al-Duwaihi and Muhammad Luqman.

At Riverhead, we learned specialized Arabic terms that would likely be needed in the workplace. For example:

"*Wain al-mutraga?*" (Where is the hammer?)

The answer: "*TaHt al-sayyarah.*" (Under the car.)

Although these terms were used primarily by blue-collar workers, we also learned the Arabic alphabet and how to pronounce the many unaccustomed sounds of the Arabic language. Exposed as well to the basics of Arab culture, we were better prepared to live and work in the Kingdom.

After Riverhead, I boarded a brand-new aircraft – a DC-6 – bound for Dhahran. It was also four-engined but was pressurized, allowing it to fly at higher altitudes, above the occasional lower-level turbulence. Aramco had purchased two DC-6s and had named them, like their predecessors, the *Flying Camel* and the *Flying Gazelle*. They were much more comfortable and a bit faster. Because the plane had a greater range, we overnighted this time in Rome instead of Portugal.

At Riverhead, the Saudi instructors had warned us many times that when we arrived in Saudi Arabia we would encounter very hot weather, humidity and frequent sandstorms. The instructors reminded me that my previous stay in Ras Tanura had been during the winter, when the weather was much cooler, but now I would be experiencing real heat.

Nevertheless, the warnings did not prepare me for the reality of an Arabian summer. When the door of the plane opened and I stepped down the ramp, I could not believe the intensity of the heat, which was magnified by the suffocating humidity. It felt almost like I was stepping into an open furnace.

In Ras Tanura, the street signs in both the refinery and the office areas were in three languages – Arabic, English and Italian. At first, the Saudi and Italian workers seemed to get along well enough. In time, however, the Saudis became critical of the Italians, calling them good craftsmen but unmotivated and not really willing to work. It became apparent early on that most of the Italian workers were homesick for their native land, felt out of place, and would not fit well with the Saudis and the Americans. The company decided to gradually phase out the Italian contingent, replacing them as soon as was practicable with Pakistanis, Indians or, even better, Saudis.

In those early years at Ras Tanura, I came to realize that the Saudi workforce would become key to the company's and my future success. I reached this conclusion despite the fact that Americans – along with Pakistanis, Indians and Italians – were at that time the primary craftsmen, plant operators and transportation-skilled employees. To replace these foreign workers at some time in the future, Aramco would need to place special emphasis on the selection, training and education of Saudi candidates who exhibited raw aptitude, intelligence and motivation.

The use of three languages at Ras Tanura led to the coining of many words that were combinations of the three. This happened most often when Saudis encountered mechanical objects or equipment for which there was no well-known Arabic word.

The Saudis would tend to take the American English word for the object and "Saudize" it with the appropriate prefixes and suffixes.

For example, there was no readily-available Arabic word for "truck." The Saudis had a well-known Arabic word for car – *sayyara* – but a truck became a *Kenwar*, because the big trucks that Aramco used for the desert were Kenworths, hardy industrial vehicles that are still made in Seattle. Thus a truck – any truck – became a *Kenwar* and they devised a plural for that, *Kenawwir* – words still in use today. There were many other colloquial Saudi words built from English roots. Tire repair shops in the Eastern Province are even today often called bunshur, from the English word "puncture." If a Saudi wanted to convey the Arabic equivalent of "You fired me," he might say "*Inta finishtnee*" (You "finished" me).

Chapter 4
Partners and Rivals

In the late 1930s and early 1940s, while war wracked the European and Pacific theaters, world oil production was growing – but from a rather small base. The United States, Venezuela, Iran, Iraq and the Caspian Sea region of the Soviet Union were the most prolific producing areas known at the time. The oil industry was expanding in these known areas as drilling and transportation technologies improved. Exploration technology was still in its infancy when Socal obtained its concession to explore from the newly-established Kingdom of Saudi Arabia.

Middle East production was primarily based in Iran and Iraq, and was dominated by British and French interests – which had not seriously competed for the concession in the virtually uncharted Arabian Peninsula, where even borders remained unclear, except for areas specifically ruled by the founder of Saudi Arabia, King Abdulaziz Al Saud.

As noted earlier, Socal discovered oil in eastern Saudi Arabia in 1933. However, it exported little crude oil until after the end of World War II. In 1946, world demand for oil was modest, with prices as low as $1.50 per barrel. The Aramco partners – Socal, Texaco, Exxon and Mobil – had by then made a significant investment in Saudi Arabia and were producing Saudi oil, at times even at the expense of their own smaller interests elsewhere. These companies were also involved at that time in Iraq and Iran.

Worldwide oil production capacity was becoming a matter of concern at this time in all the producing countries, especially those that needed additional income to cover post-war expenses. Saudi Arabia, for example, continually urged Aramco to produce more oil to help meet the country's own development needs – even if that meant the company's four partners had to reduce production elsewhere. Oil companies were hearing the same argument in the other producing countries.

Since it was a new source, Aramco's growing production at times tended to push down oil prices, which hovered in the neighborhood of $1.80 per barrel. The Saudi population was widely scattered over a country the size of the United States east of the Mississippi River, and modernization meant building highways, power grids, and communications and water systems. All of this national development required a huge system of "taxation in reverse" to get money to the people. Aramco management worked closely with the Board of Directors to determine the company's constantly-changing production needs well into the future. On average it took about five years to build a new Aramco plant, from planning to final commissioning.

Against this backdrop, in 1946 Aramco – legally structured as a Delaware-based U.S. company – became a more formalized venture with four major publicly-held American shareholders. Exxon and Mobil bought 40 percent of the company from the first two shareholders, with Exxon taking 30 percent of Aramco and Mobil 10 percent. The sale meant that three of the partners were equal owners with 30 percent each and one, Mobil, held 10 percent. It was agreed in that transaction that each of the four partners, though unequal in ownership, would have two members on the Aramco Board of Directors. Aramco could appoint five members to the Board.

In 1959, the company elected its first two Saudi directors – Abdullah H. Al-Tariki, the Kingdom's Director General of Petroleum and Mineral Resources (and later Oil Minister), and Hafiz Wahbah, a former Ambassador to the United Kingdom.

Publicly-held U.S. corporations like the Aramco shareholders were required to report their financial results quarterly, so Aramco's accounting procedures and reporting were presented to them for public inspection by their stockholders on that basis, too. The four owners were individually buyers of Aramco crude and refined products. They may have been partners in this venture, but they were also market competitors. They bought Aramco crude and products in quantities that did not necessarily match their percentage ownership, because, for example, a 30 percent owner had the right to a pro rata share of sales. Similarly both crude oil and oil products were sold by grade, with varying values. These grades were produced from different reservoirs and flowed into separate plants.

The unequal ownership percentages and differing product needs created problems, which were handled by Aramco's New York office, for many years headed by a senior vice president, J.J. "Joe" Johnston, who also managed that office and was

Aramco's New York office initiates the first direct cable link to Dhahran In 1965. Present for activation of the cable were Frank Jungers, Aramco CEO Tom Barger, and N.Y. office head Joe Johnston.

an Aramco director. This office, located at 505 Park Avenue in Manhattan, served as Aramco's liaison with the shareholder companies, three of which (all but Socal) were also headquartered in New York. In 1964, I was assigned to the New York office as assistant general manager, and I lived in Scarsdale, an upscale community in which Aramco had purchased a house for me and for subsequent executives on that training assignment in New York. (Brock Powers, who was in charge of Aramco exploration activities, followed me in this one-and-a-half-year assignment.) While the assignment was partly training, I was also asked to chair the "Study Group," made up of executive assistants representing the Board directors for each of the four shareholder companies.

The committee dealt with shareholder requirements and issues that might later become Board matters if not resolved at this level. As chairman of the Study Group, I represented Aramco's problems and requirements, which also might include Saudi Government preferences. Several members of this group later rose to much higher positions in their respective companies. For example, James Kinnear, a Study Group member for Texaco, eventually became chairman and CEO of that company. Upon retirement (and after the Saudi Government purchased Aramco), Kinnear served on the Saudi Aramco Board of Directors.

The Aramco Board met once every quarter, but it also had an Executive Committee (EXCOM), which met monthly. EXCOM was chaired by the Aramco chairman and CEO and included one director from each of the shareholder companies, as well as one Saudi Government director. EXCOM handled the declaration of monthly dividends and other matters that needed attention more quickly than the usual quarterly Board meetings. Senior vice president and director Joe Johnston was EXCOM secretary.

A second key committee was formed – ANCOM, the Committee Dealing with Aramco Negotiations with the Government. It authorized all negotiations with the Saudi Government and met as often as needed. It was also composed of one director from each shareholder company, together with the Aramco senior vice president of Concession Affairs and the chairman and CEO of Aramco. (In 1968, I became senior vice president of Concession Affairs, replacing Robert I. Brougham when he became president of Aramco.)

The matters handled by ANCOM were not discussed at Aramco Board meetings because the Saudi Government had directors on the Board, who obviously would

Aramco's cable office was located for many years in the Administration Building (North), Dhahran. Photo by A.Y. Dobais.

have had a conflict of interest. The Saudi Government was aware of ANCOM and understood the need for it. ANCOM's meeting files in Saudi Arabia, therefore, only noted approved items after they had been negotiated and agreed with the Saudi Government.

ANCOM was the vehicle that pursued negotiations with the Saudi Government to accommodate the needs of Aramco and its shareholders. At all times, however, it was important to keep in mind that the shareholder oil companies were very active competitors – all were in the downstream business of refining crude oil and marketing such refined products as gasoline, diesel, jet fuel and heavy oil. The retail markets differed from country to country throughout the world, and the brand-named products that originated in Saudi Arabia were sold to customers in highly-competitive arenas.

Thus Aramco became heavily involved with the four partners in developing a common position on negotiations with the Saudi Government. Indeed, in those cases Aramco became the shareholders' negotiator with the Government. The company therefore attempted to develop a joint, shareholder-approved negotiating stance that stood the best chance of being accepted by the Saudi Government.

Typically, the Study Group was very much involved in shareholder negotiations involving Aramco dividend allocations in those cases in which sales to shareholders deviated significantly from their ownership percentages. Aramco, of course, was aware of how product sales were allotted among the shareholders at any given time. In fact, Aramco knew what each shareholder's forecasts were for future requirements by grade of crude and type of refined product.

But Aramco could not share the individual requirements of one shareholder buyer with the others because they were indeed competitors and did not want their sales needs to be known by their partners, who might be planning acquisitions in the same area. Thus, when Aramco made up its capital expenditure forecast, it received the four partners' projected requirements secretly.

As one can imagine, we at Aramco New York often found ourselves in a difficult and delicate position, having access to confidential plans from four highly-competitive oil companies. We took this responsibility seriously and respected the requirements of confidentiality. By comparing projections, we were able to eliminate duplications arising when two companies projected a similar prospective sale. Aramco's projected capital budget would eliminate duplicate projections without informing the individual shareholders of our corrections or what had caused them. Our capital budget needs were huge – Aramco was a rapidly-growing company, with new facilities always being planned and under construction – and excess projections could greatly reduce the funds available to shareholders as dividends and to the Government as taxes.

I and my successor, Brock Powers, were in New York during a period of rapidly-increasing worldwide demand when Aramco was required to meet the dated demands of the shareholders' international markets. It was very important that we analyze these multiple demands and eliminate any duplication, so that Aramco would not build too much capacity at its facilities. During this period, the shareholders thoroughly questioned our projected requirements, out of curiosity about the competition but, more importantly, to be sure that Aramco met their own production needs.

The individual growth rates of the four partners also differed from time to time, to the point where one shareholder might want to purchase or lift more than his percentage ownership share.

For example, let's assume that Mobil, a 10 percent shareholder, wanted to lift 18 percent of a certain crude. Mobil would then have produced 18 percent of the profit, but was entitled to only 10 percent of the dividend paid on the basis of its ownership percentage. This requirement to purchase would usually result in an increased dividend for all four shareholders, but the partners would need to agree among themselves that Mobil, in this case, would receive a larger dividend for a certain period of time, after which the other partners were very likely to try to capture the same business for themselves. The Study Group generally thrashed out this complex negotiation, for eventual approval by ANCOM.

To sum up, then: The four Aramco owners were competitors with unequal ownership but equal Board seats and voting rights. They were publicly-held companies who reported to their shareholders quarterly and as such were watchful of quarterly earnings and other quarterly measurements. Aramco, which they jointly owned, reported quarterly as well. Aramco operated the concession business: It found, extracted and exported the oil, paid the host government taxes and royalties, paid expenses, financed capital programs and paid out the remainder as dividends to the owners.

Later, as leaders of countries in the developing world began to think about owning or nationalizing foreign companies operating in their countries, especially those exporting the country's precious natural resources, a distinct change in management goals of oil companies in such countries began to emerge worldwide. Financial emphasis was becoming more long-range. Mandatory quarterly reporting would no longer be required once the business came under government ownership. And the long-range protection of resources became a bigger issue, and the responsibility of management. Aramco was inexorably being pulled into a different strategic outlook.

Chapter 5
Aramcons: Forging a Workforce

Aramco began to grow rapidly in the late 1940s, and expanding the workforce became the major challenge. The company urgently needed all kinds of craftsmen, producing and refining operators, transportation, marine and heavy equipment operators, mechanics, geologists, petroleum engineers, drillers and many other skilled workers. It also needed administrative personnel and large numbers of clerical workers – keep in mind that there were no office computers in those early days, and very little automation of paperwork. Teachers, typists, nurses, medical personnel, and telephone and wireless technicians were badly needed as well. The company hired Americans to fill specialist technical and lead blue-collar positions, all of which were very costly. To attract U.S. employees, the company offered such inducements as family housing, schools and other amenities including retail food centers, restaurants and quality medical facilities, along with lengthy and costly biennial vacation leaves.

American hires were therefore kept to the essential minimum and supplemented by skilled employees of other nationalities closer to Saudi Arabia who could be hired on "bachelor status" – without accompanying family members. Recruitment efforts focused first on Italians from Eritrea, and then on Indians and Pakistanis, Sudanese and Palestinians. Questions arose immediately as to the best ways to handle the needs of these different cultures. Should they be separated by nationality or by their

An all-Saudi oil crew poses before the Shedgum No. 12 rig near Ain Dar in 1953. Photo by Owen Oxley.

education and job levels, which varied widely? To what extent should they be trained? Decisions had to be made about which nationalities would be offered permanent employment before some of these problems could be answered. Obviously, for the long term, Saudis and Americans were viewed as the main pool of career employees. In time, they became the first "Aramcons."

In 1944-45, more than 2,000 Italian civilian workers were recruited from Eritrea, where they had remained as the residue of the Italian presence after British forces defeated Mussolini's army in Italian East Africa. Aramco opened a recruiting office in Asmara, the capital of Eritrea, where stranded Italian craftsmen of all trades were waiting for an opportunity to return to Italy as World War II drew to an end. All trades were recruited, including electricians, welders, pipefitters, carpenters, mechanics, masons, and even draftsmen and engineers.

Italians, like other non-American foreigners, were hired on "bachelor status." Since the Italians' families were not with them in Eritrea, they were not included in the regular Aramco hiring arrangements. The Italians lived in two tented bachelor camps – Ras Tanura Camp and Al-Azizia Camp, close to, but outside, the family communities of Ras Tanura and Dhahran, respectively. They had their own Italian kitchen staff, entertainers and recreation facilities. At times they invited their American friends to parties and dinners. When the weather was cool enough, they held boxing matches and outdoor movies, and imported flowers, fresh fruit and other products from Asmara.

The American supervisory craft foremen had mixed feelings about their Italian employees – work results were spotty because, as mentioned earlier, the Italians frequently got along poorly with the Saudis and the other foreigners in their crews. They were also ineffective in training lower-level employees of any nationality. In retrospect, the Italian workers, for a variety of reasons, including their desire to return home to Italy, really had very little motivation to train others – especially since, for the most part, they did not speak English and were not qualified as trainers.

As it happened, an electrical foreman in Ras Tanura, Bob Thomas, had a large crew of Italian power-line workers assisted by Saudi helpers. The crew as a whole was very hard-working and the most productive of all the refinery crews in my maintenance workforce. One day I asked Bob how he had been so successful in motivating these Italians. He replied that he had read that Italians liked colorful, flashy uniforms. So he had bought them nice blue shirts, and his wife Betty sewed gold stripes on the sleeves every time they performed well. Bob said they strove competitively for the most stripes and were very proud of them.

Some Italian employees were unusual characters – particularly one named Ilo Battigelli, a draftsman at Ras Tanura who happened to be a highly-talented amateur photographer. He called himself "Ilo the Pirate," in part because his photo studio was located on a beach where corsairs had once landed, and partly because he was a romantic by nature. He played on his own eccentricity by dressing up as a typical haughty pirate with colorful split-sleeve shirts, flannel shorts, big earrings and a hat fashioned by tying the corners of a bandana in knots. His photographs, mostly black and white, were varied, creative and classic shots of Arab and American subjects, as well as everyday Saudi life. Battigelli's photographic accomplishments have been recognized internationally, and his work has appeared in a number of major books on the Kingdom.

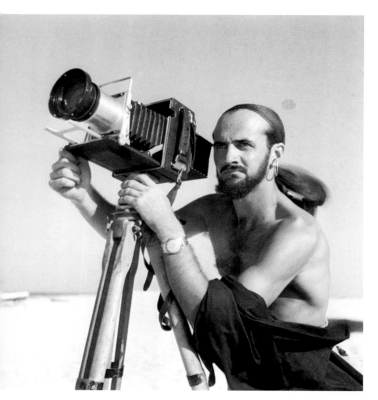

Ilo Battigelli, a Ras Tanura draftsman who gained fame as a photographer. He was known as "Ilo the Pirate." "The 24-year-old transformed himself into Ilo the Pirate partly because his studio was on a beach where, according to legend, corsairs used to land, and partly because of his own romantic flair." Al-Ayyam Al-Jamilah magazine, Fall 2005. Photo courtesy of Danielle Battigelli Rogers.

The Italian workforce dwindled by the late 1950s, as more and more of the workers were able to return to their home country. Due to Asmara's popularity with the Italians and the colorful stories they told about it, the Eritrean capital became a regular watering hole for Aramco's American workers and their families for a number of years. Asmara, sitting about 4,000 feet above sea level, was cool and sunny, with beautiful gardens and flowers and a good sprinkling of small hotels, inns and restaurants, along with wines and spirits unobtainable in the Kingdom. It turned out to be a great spot for a short vacation!

Palestinians were much in demand as training instructors in classrooms and craft training centers for Saudi employees. The Palestinians who joined Aramco were well educated, versatile and bilingual. Many of them had experience as technicians in a variety of communications facilities, machine shops and laboratories. The Saudi Government encouraged Aramco to hire at least 1,000 Palestinians, in part to help relieve the difficult conditions of Palestinians living in exile in refugee camps.

Aramco hired Indians, Pakistanis and Sudanese, primarily as craftsmen and helpers before Saudis had received sufficient education and training to be hired for these positions. Most of them came from areas in their countries that had been under British rule or administration, and thus had fair English-language skills, even if their educational levels were low. Their specialized craft skills were often not up to American standards, but they were certainly better than raw, unskilled labor.

In 1952, I was appointed supervisor of all maintenance and shops work at Ras Tanura Refinery, as well at the storage and shipping terminal that handled all tanker exports of crude oil and refined products. There were about 3,000 craftsman and laborers involved, each trade under an American foreman. We also maintained all residential housing and office facilities.

I had been doing engineering design work for the refinery and terminal during my first four-plus years with the company. I was familiar with the plant facilities but I had little direct supervisory experience. So I decided to start things off by getting to know the foremen and understanding the work of each craft, along with their capabilities, workload and assignment systems. I spent little or no time on day-to-day problems or needs.

After two or three weeks, I came to my office one morning and found that the general foreman of steel workers and boilermakers, one Louis E. "Pinky" Schlosa, was waiting to see me. Pinky was a burly, powerful, deep-voiced man from Wyoming, who was well respected by his peers. He was easily old enough to be my father. He had on a new white shirt for the occasion and as he sat down in front of my desk, his thick fingers were shaking as he pulled out some crumpled notepaper from his pocket. He fumbled with the paper a bit and finally spoke.

"You've been here for a couple of weeks looking around, but, Frank – look, we have work to do," he said. "We need some answers and choices, so we can get going. A 'yes' is as good as a 'no'! Just pick one, so that we can move forward."

He got up and, as he was leaving, turned around and said: "I'll help ya!"

That turned out to be one of the most useful lessons in the art of supervision that I ever learned – it gave me confidence and made me more decisive.

As time went by, with the workload growing rapidly, I better understood the potential output of the various crafts. I could appreciate the frustrations of the individual American craftsmen, who felt that they were short-handed and needed more and better helpers.

In addition to American and Italian craftsmen, the work crews contained three basic grades of workers:

- *Intermediate grade*: Skilled craftsmen with a working grasp of English.
- *General grade*: Helpers with minimum craft experience, able to undergo part-time oral training in their chosen craft in English.
- *Laborers*: Saudis in part-time English classes and introductory training in basic overall work skills, including safety.

The general grade helpers were nearly all foreigners (mostly Muslim Pakistanis). Some of the brightest were receiving specific craft training with the objective of reaching intermediate grade and full craft skills and thus minimizing the hiring of expensive American craftsmen. A few exceptional Saudis were beginning to break through into intermediate status.

The foremen and the craftsmen preferred to hire more general-level Pakistanis, along with more craft trainers, and temporarily slow the hiring of Saudis – because they felt the Saudis were taking too long to achieve the needed craft skills.

Personally, I concluded it was unwise to hire more foreign helpers who would need additional training for eventual promotion, even though they might require fewer instructors and would thus free up more instructors to accelerate the training of Saudis. But we all agreed that we needed to develop a training program that contained the precise steps required in each of the different crafts to train a Saudi laborer to become a helper and eventually a full craftsman. We asked each craft foreman to develop a step-by-step training program to be taught by an American craftsman, who would then report the trainees' progress on a check-off sheet.

Within months, the Saudi trainees showed enough promise that everyone agreed no more foreign helpers needed to be hired. Shortly after that, there was reluctant agreement not to renew any foreign helper contracts. Foreigners could be promoted only if there were roster openings for full craftsman and if no Saudis were available and qualified for promotion.

While some in Aramco management felt we were moving too quickly, various other areas in the company, such as the production and drilling departments, began to follow suit, given the clear need to hire local help wherever possible. Our approach began to pay off in another way, too – by minimizing the social problems of feeding, housing and providing leave for lower-level foreign employees.

Early on, it was clear that the blue-collar Americans and the Saudi workers got along well, because they seemed to have the same sort of independent attitude. The Saudis, like the Americans, usually said what they thought and were not afraid to speak up. The straight-talking, blue-collar Americans liked the Saudis for that.

Naturally problems arose – social frictions and rivalries – when the various levels of employees were brought together. At first, the lowest grades were Saudis – they were starting off with absolutely no experience in industrial activities that their country had never seen before. The employees at the next level, who had more education and skills – especially clerical and white-collar workers – were nearly all foreigners, and were housed in an intermediate camp, which had better facilities than existed in the general camp where the lower-level blue-collar and general Saudi labor lived. On the positive side, the promotion ladder for the first time offered promise to the lower-level workers, and the Saudi laborers at Ras Tanura knew that the more education and training they received, and the more experience they accumulated, the more employee benefits they would enjoy.

Saudi employees eagerly sought increased and more specific job-skill training, which was then initiated in the craft and operating jobs, in addition to the basic academic schooling already being provided.

Job-skill requirements had to be outlined very specifically and taught for each of the skills and crafts involved. The training was assigned to American craftsmen, who may not have been trained as teachers but were experts in the skills of their positions.

In many cases, top Saudi craftsmen who had learned their skills well and shown leadership potential were sent to trade and technical schools in the United States. This effort produced results quickly as these employees realized that with their training and experience they could attain jobs previously filled only by foreigners.

It is interesting to consider what kinds of Saudis and what kinds of Americans came together and worked under the new and expanding – in fact, pioneering – umbrella of Aramco. In the process, Saudis and Americans learned a great deal about each other and their respective cultures and homelands.

The Americans came mostly from the oilfields and refineries of Texas and California – they were tough workers who understood long hours and hard work. Later they were joined by craftsmen and others from the drought-stricken farm areas of the Midwest, who were looking for steady work. These employees were often from remote, sparsely-populated states like Wyoming, North Dakota and Oklahoma. Many were recent graduates with technical degrees who needed work and money – myself included. A few women teachers, nurses and clerical personnel also began to arrive from the same locales. All in all, these new hires were an adventurous sort who understood hard work, looked forward to world travel opportunities and were intrigued by the challenges and pioneering spirit found in Aramco and Saudi Arabia.

One could draw some parallels with the Saudi employees, who in the beginning included many Bedouins from the Najd and from the northeastern deserts of Saudi Arabia. A good number of these were from tribes that had once roamed free but had been brought to rein by King Abdulaziz in his unification of the Kingdom. Early on, these Bedouin "free spirits" were employed as desert guides and workers in geological crews. After the company struck oil and began to expand, those with leadership potential who were unencumbered by families or other dependents became truck drivers, mechanics and oilfield workers – all supervised and trained by American blue-collar craftsmen while going to school part-time.

As the workforce grew, other Saudis from the Eastern Province – from towns like Qatif and Safwa and from the great oasis of Al-Hasa – were hired as camp workers, to be trained as masons, carpenters, plumbers, electricians, cooks and domestic help. Although their families lived nearby, they too were young men who needed work and were adventurous enough to learn such new and unknown skills as might attract their interest. Many very young men – even boys willing to fudge on their ages – scrambled to get on the Aramco payroll, where they could go to training classes in English and elementary studies.

Perhaps it would be useful to consider what kinds of Americans and Saudis were not attracted to these new, intriguing and unusual jobs in a pioneering venture far from home.

In the case of the Americans, very few of the new hires came from New York or the Eastern Seaboard or from that region's distinguished Ivy League universities. Nor did they come from the cotton and tobacco farms of the Southeast, or from Southern "Bible Belt" states like Mississippi and Alabama, or from industrialized ones like Michigan, Illinois and Ohio, or from the film and entertainment areas of Hollywood and Los Angeles. Somewhat similarly, few Saudis came from the commercial areas around Jeddah or the religious and intellectual areas of Mecca and Medina. The people of these cities had much less interest in leaving home. The same applied to Saudis from the central area of Al-Qassim and its main cities of Buraida and Unaiza –

Frank Jungers, as General Superintendent, Engineering and Maintenance Supply in Dhahran in April 1959. Photo by V K. Antony.

few from the conservative central Arabian heartland were interested in working with foreigners outside their traditional communities.

While, as we have seen, Saudis and Americans generally got along well at work, Aramco management faced many problems related to the types of housing acceptable to workers of each nationality, some of whom had to live in tents. Providing housing acceptable to all was a continual challenge. Things became more complicated as lower-level employees advanced to higher-paying jobs. Not surprisingly, these employees began asking for dormitories with running water, electricity and other amenities – even though they may have grown up living in tents without such facilities. Saudis from nearby towns tended to live at home with their families, but they needed daily transportation. Those who lived in distant Al-Hasa were satisfied with bachelor accommodations but they needed weekend transportation back to their homes. This meant setting up a bus system, and building roads across the desert to accommodate those buses (as well as other vehicles).

Thus, in all three early Aramco communities – at headquarters in Dhahran, near the refining and terminal area of Ras Tanura and in the major producing area of Abqaiq, south of Dhahran – lower-level Saudi workers lived in bachelor dormitories and were bussed home for their days off. Craftsmen and white-collar workers – mostly South Asians, Sudanese and other foreigners – were housed in intermediate bachelor quarters that were superior in quality and more private. This system proved satisfactory until the Saudi employees climbed up in the ranks, acquiring more skills and thus earning better quarters. At this point, large numbers of Saudi employees started asking for better living quarters and Aramco's housing policies began to come into question. The next chapter will explore the ways the company sought to resolve these problems.

Chapter 6
Providing for Our Workers

In some respects, the problems faced by a new nation were also the problems of a new company. Providing suitable housing and living amenities for a number of differing cultures in a multi-skilled workforce is a difficult problem on its own. It was made even more onerous for Aramco because the new Kingdom of Saudi Arabia was just starting out on the road to national development and the local infrastructure of the Eastern Province was totally incapable of providing for the employee support needs of a large international industrial enterprise. Financial and monetary services were virtually nonexistent, as was the infrastructure needed to house, feed and generally care for the influx of foreign workers, families and others. We needed to keep in mind that, as we built our company and cared for our workers' needs, we were also helping to build the young Kingdom, providing it with practical lessons and useful tools for national development.

The company provided separate housing for most of the lower-level expatriate craft workers because there were no available accommodations in the local towns and these workers could not be housed with Saudis, who lived either with their families or as bachelors. Many Saudis, having limited experience of international contact, were uncomfortable with the idea of living with foreigners, particularly foreigners they regarded as less skilled than themselves. Lower-level foreign craft workers often practiced different religions from the Muslim Saudis, and in any case their customs and cultures were usually quite different from those of the Arabian Peninsula, so it made sense to provide them with separate housing arrangements, often in dormitories or other common facilities.

This practice also created some discord, because the company wanted to keep the housing amenities somewhat equal between Saudi workers and other general employees.

On the job, the Saudis, after minimal training, began to feel they were being discriminated against because the foreigners seemed to have better jobs. These feelings naturally became intertwined with status: What housing was correct and appropriate for each employee's different needs? What kinds of transportation should be provided? And what about differing training needs? As previously noted, we quickly realized that we should be spending as little time as possible training foreigners, concentrating instead on training Saudis – who were, after all, in the broadest sense, the company's hosts and its long-term future.

Other on-the-job issues arose almost immediately. Here are some examples.

Prayer Time

The Saudis, as Muslims firmly committed to the observances of their faith, required time off from work to pray five times a day. Two of these prayers – the noon (*dhuhr*) and afternoon (*'asr*) prayers – occurred during normal working hours. The company allowed breaks for prayer time even when work was in progress, and employees were permitted to decide exactly how to time those breaks, as they felt appropriate. The prayer breaks lasted about 20–30 minutes.

Muslim employees could leave the workplace and go to an appropriate location to pray if they so chose. Of course some did – going to the nearest mosque (*masjid*) or prayer area (*musalla*), or praying individually or in small groups – and some did not.

Islam also permits flexibility in prayer times, so it was not unusual for an employee to finish an important task on the job before taking time off to pray. Most Saudis did pray, however, and that was something Americans had to learn to honor and accommodate. Corresponding time off was not allowed for non-Muslim employees, who had no such prayer obligations – they continued working during Muslim prayer time.

Payday and Silver Coins

Originally there was a shortage of currency in our work communities, which presented a number of difficulties. In early days, Indian rupee coins and paper bills were used in the communities because the Saudi Government did not have sufficient national coinage available. The Saudi one riyal coin (valued at around 3.7 riyals per dollar) was the Kingdom's largest denomination and was also in short supply. Later, as time went on, the Saudis did mint more and more silver coins, but not in larger denominations. In the beginning, there was no paper riyal currency.

Thus the Saudi workforce had to be paid in silver riyal coins, which became a serious burden because the coins had to be counted out and checked by hand. Saudi employees were given this coinage in sacks, with a slip of paper designating what they

Payday: an employee in the Accounting Office readies 2,000 silver Saudi riyal coins. Dhahran, 1947.

had earned. Each employee had to verify the count before he left the pay window. In the later 1940s, the payroll amounted to over U.S.$5 million per month, which translated to some 60 metric tons of coins, which had to be delivered from storage to payroll points on flatbed trucks and then physically handed out.

Friday was – and of course is – the Muslim holy day, corresponding to Sunday in Christian society. Thus Friday was a day off and employees worked on Saturday and Sunday. Thursday, then, became payday. The Saudi workers were usually paid weekly or bi-weekly. The process took a lot of time, and usually the pay period began around noon: During the afternoon they received their pay and then went home for the weekend.

Later, as the workforce expanded, additional time was needed to distribute the sacks of coins, and so finally payday, Thursday, became a full day off similar to the Western Saturday, not only in Arabia but also in most of the Muslim world. (This has changed in recent years, as most Muslim countries, including almost all of Saudi Arabia's Gulf neighbors, have switched from the Thursday-Friday weekend to Friday-Saturday, bringing their schedules into closer alignment with the rest of the world. Oman switched to the Friday, Saturday weekend in May 2013 and following a vote by the Shura Council or consultative assembly Saudi Arabia also adopted a Friday-Saturday weekend from late July 2013.

In 1961, the Saudi Government introduced riyal paper currency for general use, along with personal banking, and Aramco's lengthy coin payroll exercise came to a welcome end.

"Slugs": Royalty Payments in Gold

Another payment issue: The Saudi Government had stipulated in the Concession Agreement that petroleum royalties were to be paid in gold. Hence in the early years, as production began and shipments of oil were exported from the Kingdom, the resulting royalties were paid in gold coinage commonly available in the region. The British gold sovereign, weighing a bit less than a quarter of an ounce and minted internationally as bullion for centuries, was the logical coin of preference. Aramco spent a great deal of time locating and buying gold sovereigns to make these payments. There were no large banks in the area, and the coinage had to be delivered to the Saudi Treasury in Riyadh by truck.

The obverse and reverse of a gold bullion disk minted in Philadelphia and used by Aramco to pay royalties to Saudi Government.

As oil production grew, of course, the requirement for gold sovereigns increased and gold coins became scarcer, so the company arranged for the Philadelphia Mint to produce gold bullion in the form of coin-like discs to make these royalty payments in lieu of actual coinage. The gold discs bore the U.S. eagle and the legend "U.S. Mint, Philadelphia, USA" on one side and three lines of data about fineness and weight on the other. "They looked like coins, they were used as coins, but, technically, they weren't coins," said *Aramco World* magazine in a 1981 article.[1] The gold discs, popularly known to the American workforce as "slugs," were acceptable to the Saudi Government as bullion, of course. Since one gold disc weighed about four times as much as a gold sovereign, they reduced the number of gold pieces required and eliminated the need to scour the world gold market for sovereigns. But this system of royalty payment did remain something of a chore until the 1950s, when the Kingdom established a modern banking system and royalties were paid in the conventional manner, through bank transfers. The discs could not be used as coins, but many people did buy them as they came onto the market and kept them as souvenirs or collectibles.

---

[1] Robert Obojski, "A Special Luster," *Aramco World*, Sep/Oct 1981.

Noontime Meals

In the early years, there was considerable discussion among management and employees about what the work schedule should be, especially in the hot summer months. In the company's camp at Abqaiq, in the heart of the oil-producing area, summer daytime temperatures could hit 50° C (122° F). Summer working conditions were especially difficult for employees in such heat-generating areas as refineries and producing plants.

Saudi employees were new to the oil industry's intensive work regime. Many were not yet comfortable with the workload, in part because they were not getting enough nourishment to perform strenuous physical labor in the heat.

When the Saudis came to work in the morning, they brought their own lunches, which in most cases were very minimal – a few dates and a little rice, perhaps – not enough nourishment to sustain a hard-working person throughout the day. So the company established noontime meal facilities in some of the larger work areas, where

Employees order lunch at new Abqaiq cafeteria in 1956.

Saudi employees could get hot, nourishing food that would keep them going through the rest of the workday. The lunchtime facilities were well received at first but soon employees began using them less and less, for at least two reasons.

First of all, the Saudi employees did not particularly like the food. This was partly because they were not used to the Western menu and partly, perhaps, because the food was not as tasty as it might have been.

Secondly, it turned out that the employees were resisting the idea of accepting free food, which they thought amounted to begging. In short, the Saudi employees were insulted to receive what amounted to a "handout," and this became an important reason not to visit these lunchtime establishments.

At one point, some employees staged something of a food-related "sit-in" at Ras Tanura. The company made a serious effort to transform these noontime meal stations into something more acceptable. Menus were changed and improved, and augmented as necessary. Then a minimum price was charged for the meal, which went over well when Saudi employees were given a pay raise to cover the added expense of lunch. They could then choose whether or not to buy their midday meals. Later, we noticed that these company-provided lunches began to positively influence their home-prepared diets as well, by encouraging consumption of healthful fresh vegetables, fruits and the like.

Many other workers, including the Pakistanis, also ate at these noontime "restaurants." These non-Saudi workers had dining facilities at their residential quarters as well, for morning and evening meals. Due to cultural differences, the company provided separate areas in the residential dining facilities for Saudis and for other foreign workers. The American professionals either ate their meals at home or at company "dining halls" equivalent to normal Western restaurants. In the early days, due to menu preferences and cultural differences, blue-collar Saudi workers did not eat at these dining halls. Nevertheless, Aramco management continued to debate the question of whether dining facilities should be consolidated or separate facilities continued for each employee category, by pay grade or nationality. As it turned out, in the smaller communities dining facilities became more and more combined as time went on. The feeding and care of employees was an ever-continuing task, not only for community-service facilities but also for their staff – waiters, cooks and the like.

Shi'ite and Sunni Workers

The company discovered that the workers best suited for the jobs in these community facilities – restaurants and indeed all other community services – seemed to be the Shi'ite Muslim employees, most of whom lived in the Qatif area opposite the islands of Bahrain, whose population was also mostly Shi'ite.

Shi'ites belong to the second largest branch of the Islamic faith, often called Shi'a Islam. *Shi'a* in Arabic means "faction" and refers to the faction supporting Ali, the Prophet Muhammad's son-in-law. The other branch of Islam is larger in numbers of adherents and is called Sunni Islam. Shi'ites regard Ali and his descendants as the legitimate successors to Muhammad. Iran is home to the world's largest Shi'ite population, estimated at some 70 million. Saudi Arabia hosts a Shi'ite minority community numbering about 3–4 million in a total Saudi population of about 28 million; the largest Shi'ite population is in the Eastern Province.

From the beginning, Aramco was acutely aware of compatibility issues between Sunni and Shi'ite Muslims. The Shi'ites were definitely in the minority nationally but made up a majority in the Eastern Province, and tended to live in separate areas. The company was very careful, as a matter of policy, not to allow this religious difference to become a factor in the training or evaluation of an employee. Men from both branches became Aramcons, and in my experience the Sunni–Shi'ite question rarely came up in the workforce. In the Dhahran district maintenance and transportation shops workforce that I supervised in the 1950s, Abdul Moniem ibn Abdullah, a Shi'ite, was promoted to foreman of the Welding and Sheet metal shop. He was a trained craftsman and the first Saudi foreman in Dhahran to replace an American. This shop happened to be predominately Sunni. His appointment was readily accepted by his co-workers and was seen as a welcome improvement over the previous, unpopular American foreman.

Problems of "Ageing"

Other problems arose that were related directly or indirectly to coordination between the Western (or Gregorian) calendar and the Islamic (or Hijri) calendar. The Hijri calendar year, based on lunar months, ends up being approximately 11 days shorter than the solar-based Western calendar year. Initially, when we were hiring Saudis, the minimum age for hire was deemed to be 18 years. Most of the Saudis, especially the Bedouin, really did not know how old they were and if they did, it was usually a Hijri year count. Most of the applicants did not have any written proof of their age.

The lunar calendar is still important in Saudi Arabia, particularly for calculating the dates of religious events, such as the beginning of the holy fasting month of Ramadan and the 'Id al-Fitr holiday that follows it.

While much attention was given to coordinating between the two calendars and figuring out exactly how old Saudi employees were, special efforts were also made to get everyone thinking in terms of the internationally-accepted Gregorian calendar and also the 24-hour clock. This became another point where Western and Middle Eastern cultures found a need to come together. On the Hijri calendar, Muslim holidays were said to begin at dawn, and dawn was determined by the ability to see a thread or a hair held up in the morning light. This point in time was regarded as the beginning of the holiday in question. This tradition was very old, dating back to the days when tribes wandered the deserts. From its very beginnings, Aramco respected this kind of cultural difference. Primary Muslim holidays were honored.

Nassir M. Al-Ajmi was a Saudi employee who came from essentially Bedouin stock and who was brought up in the desert. He went through the Aramco training program, rose up through the transportation side of the business, and eventually became an executive vice president and Board member. He once remarked that "Aramco is almost like another planet, like another culture. Aramco was part of the other culture which was a mixture of the two and not the cause."

Saudis who wanted to be hired by Aramco – especially the brightest or those with parents trying to get them a job – would claim that they were 18, the minimum hiring age. Most of them would not know what 18 actually meant in those early days, but they were nonetheless 18! When asked their age, they would say: "*Yimkin* 18." (*Yimkin* means "maybe.")

Later on, this became a problem when Aramco began to establish such things as an age-related retirement benefit. Some of our specialists in the medical department decided that they could probably tell the age of Saudi employees by X-raying their arms and analyzing their wrist bones. So a major program was initiated to X-ray employees' wrists, and from these X-rays the specialist determined what the employee's age was. This method became known as "ageing." In those early years, everyone on the Saudi payroll was "aged" in this manner and his benefits were computed accordingly.

Many employees contested their age. A "*Yimkin* 18" who was hired and thus had his birthdate set as 18 years prior to hiring might challenge this date by producing alternative evidence, such as testimony from a relative.

In later years, those approaching retirement age who wished to continue working might claim that they were actually younger and that their original "ageing" was wrong. For quite a number of years, this was an ongoing personnel problem – to determine an employee's actual age in a workforce whose cultural traditions placed little value on the precise date of birth. Later, as the workforce became more educated and the Saudi public realized that age was an important factor in determining retirement and benefits, ages were recorded by families and the "ageing" problem gradually went away.

Chapter 7
Responding to Grievances

In 1948, neither Aramco nor the Saudi Government was very well equipped to handle labor complaints from a fast-growing, untrained workforce. As we and the Government continued to grow side by side, we both learned useful lessons about how to deal with the needs of Saudi workers.

Many Saudi employees were receiving part-time training while they continued working at their jobs. These employees, as well as other full-time workers, were not shy about voicing complaints or presenting requests to their supervisors, usually Americans or other foreigners who had received little policy guidance. If the Saudi employee failed to receive satisfaction from his supervisor, he had little recourse other than to seek help from a local government official, who invariably had little experience in such matters either.

Some minor work disputes erupted that year and dissatisfaction among local employees escalated over the next few years, resulting in a wider Saudi work stoppage at Aramco. The Saudi Government quickly began discussions and entered into negotiations with Aramco to resolve these disputes and establish effective and responsive employee policies.

At that point, Aramco created an Employee Relations Group, both to develop new policies and to resolve employee problems before they became too difficult to control. Company management wanted to implement a program that would reflect best practices in corporate America for handling wage issues, labor complaints and benefits. It was important to us that these efforts should be consistent with Saudi Government policy and that they should conform to the Kingdom's laws. Along with others, I began to believe that the company needed an outlet for these complaints, a mechanism that would settle real differences but also give us better insights into what sorts of policies we needed to serve our unique workforce and to bring all employees together as one corporate "family." The company called upon a number of American and Saudi HR personnel to devise a grievance procedure whereby an employee could voice a complaint beyond his immediate supervisor if he thought such action was necessary.

A grievance procedure was drawn up, setting forth the steps an employee needed to take when escalating his complaint beyond his immediate supervisor. The first step was a visit to Employee Relations, where the aggrieved person would state his complaint and explain the reasons for it. If a supervisor or a fellow employee was involved, that person had to be identified, so that Employee Relations could bring the two together and if possible have them talk out their differences. Of course, the ideal situation would be for the ER staff to learn about a workplace grievance early in the process and target it for resolution before employees felt the need to take action.

If the Employee Relations staff failed to satisfy the employee, he had the right to see the next-level supervisor and to voice his complaint at that level. The complaint did not need to be submitted in writing. The new procedure allowed the aggrieved employee to go, step by step, up through his organization, as high in the company as he felt necessary to voice his complaint – even to the chairman of the Board, if he so chose.

The procedure became well accepted by the local workforce, and it was rarely abused once the aggrieved employee came to understand the goal of the process – to try to settle issues and problems at the lowest level possible, for his own good and that of the company.

Some very good ideas emerged from this grievance procedure, and a very high percentage of employees felt that they had been heard, even if they might not have "won" their case. Later on, when I became chairman, I remember two or three such complaints about company actions that reached my level – actions that I found no reason to reverse.

I dealt with employee grievances at many levels of my career with Aramco. After a period of time had elapsed, I would occasionally run across one of these aggrieved employees. Usually these were friendly encounters, and some were quite amusing.

One that comes to mind was a driver of our specially-designed Kenworth desert trucks. This was a highly-skilled job, well paid and much desired. Driving these mammoth trucks to remote exploration sites, sometimes over little more than a trail in the sand, was a prestigious job for any driver.

As noted in an earlier chapter, the different sounds and pronunciations of Arabic made it hard for a Saudi to say the word "Kenworth," and the pronunciation was Arabized – "*Kenwar*" and the plural "*Kenawwir*" are still popular terms in the Eastern Province for all large-sized trucks.

This particular driver – who was a Bedouin, as most truckers were in those days, and a very big man – had engaged in some clearly unsafe driving practices and therefore had been fired. But he had insisted on going up the management chain, level after level, to voice his complaints about the whole affair. As it turned out, he had been fired by none other than Nassir Al-Ajmi, who later became an executive vice president and a director of the company. During this period, Al-Ajmi was head of a portion of Aramco's Transportation Department – this was when his talents had first drawn the attention of higher management and he had begun his remarkable rise in the company. The case of the unsafe Bedouin driver came to my desk from Al-Ajmi's department. After hearing the driver's grievance, I upheld his termination.

A few years later, I was walking down the street in the nearby town of Al-Khobar one weekend when I heard a shout behind me. A big Saudi was yelling: "Jonger! Jonger!"

I stopped and turned – I recognized his face but I couldn't place him. The man said, "Don't you know me?" I replied that I recognized him but couldn't recall his name.

"*Inta finishtnee!*" he said.[1]

---

[1] For the translation and explanation, see the end of Chapter 3.

So I had fired him!

"Oh yes, I remember," I said, speaking a bit apprehensively, not knowing where this conversation would go.

"You know," said the Saudi, "you did me a big favor. I now have three trucks of my own. I don't need to work for people if I don't want to."

Then he added: "By the way, we have the same grievance procedure in my little company: It's a good thing." We laughed and shook hands.

I had not "finished" him, as it turns out. He had only just begun.

Chapter 8
Tom Barger and Home Ownership

In the early 1950s, Aramco took many steps – when necessary, with the help of the Government – to make better use of Saudis in the workforce and to integrate them more effectively into the company's Western-style business culture. Another imperative at the time was related to Saudi Arabia's national development – we needed to integrate local business communities with Aramco's operations, so that Saudi society and the economy outside Aramco moved forward alongside our large and growing Saudi workforce.

Basically the Aramco enterprise needed to establish itself in the Eastern Province – and indeed throughout the Kingdom as a whole – as a good corporate citizen that supported the development of the population. Aramco's employment needs were large enough to draw job candidates from all areas of the Kingdom. Thus the broad changes in lifestyle and aspirations required by the growing workforce were being felt throughout the Kingdom, and not just in the Eastern Province.

During this early period, Aramco management did a great deal of strategic thinking and planning on how to align the company's needs and practices with the Kingdom's aspirations for society as a whole. From the beginning, the King and the Government saw the need for nationwide infrastructure in order to meet not only Aramco's requirements but also the needs of the Saudi people, who lived in a vast peninsula that was rapidly requiring roads, communications, ports and facilities to move goods and services to isolated towns and provinces.

People who only a short time ago were essentially isolated from the outside world were now being exposed to unheard-of wonders and changes. Those of us who had just become aware of desert life learned very soon that news traveled quickly and widely in this austere environment. People in the desert passed on news, opinions and information by word of mouth, promptly and accurately. Travel across these harsh, expansive stretches of sand, scrub, lava beds and gravel, whether on foot or by camel, may have been slow but it was continuous. Indeed this kind of travel was the primary method of communication and infrastructure link when King Abdulaziz Al Saud unified the tribes of the Arabian Peninsula only a few years prior to the establishment of Aramco.

Thomas C. Barger, Aramco Chairman and CEO, 1961-69.

In the 1950s, Aramco management, primarily under the leadership of Norman "Cy" Hardy and Thomas C. Barger, realized that they needed to develop appropriate programs to attract and train a Saudi workforce and to provide them with aspirations and a lifestyle that would fit Aramco's needs.

Cy Hardy had come in from a shareholder company, Socal, and had previously worked at a high level in its foreign operations, chiefly in South and Central America. He had never been posted in the Middle East and had never before worked in a desert environment, where needs were starkly different and resources less readily available. Huge deserts simply did not provide food, water and other basics as amply as the lands in which Hardy had worked. The climate was harsher here, and society not nearly as exposed to modern development and foreign customs.

Hardy was well aware that major accommodations were needed – and quickly. He knew that his past experience was not totally suited to this environment. He chose Tom Barger as his second in command because Barger had developed a strong interest in and aptitude for Arabian culture – he admired the solid, resourceful peninsular Arab, who along with his religious beliefs and his survival skills had a strong sense of personal values of right and wrong.

Barger, who was born in Minneapolis and raised and educated in North Dakota, had come to Saudi Arabia in 1937 as a geologist but, from 1941 on, became more and more involved in dealing with Saudi communities and authorities, and with creating an Aramco Government Relations Department.[1] (He became president of Aramco in 1959, and CEO in 1961.)

Barger understood that Aramco needed to harmonize the best of Saudi and American cultures if the company was to succeed. The cultural gap was immense. At the very beginning of this relationship, the average Saudi – and American – had no idea how huge this gap really was.

The first Aramco exploration activities were undertaken by rugged geologists who crisscrossed the desert, first by camel and later by motor vehicle, studying the surface of the concession area in search of clues and indicators suggesting the presence of crude oil. By the mid-1930s, as they took their exploration effort farther and farther afield, they realized there were many possible oil prospects in this vast country – the area to be covered was so large that they needed airplanes to conduct aerial surveys.

At that point they brought in by dhow from Bahrain a Ford Trimotor aircraft – a "Tin Goose" – which they unloaded on the beach in boxes and proceeded to put

---

[1] Thomas A. Pledge, *Saudi Aramco and Its People: A History of Training.* Dhahran: 1998, pp. 83–84.

together.[2] Barger, with his interest in the Arabic language, had made great efforts to get to know the local Arabs and had become familiar with the tribes in the area where the plane was being assembled. On the day the aircraft was finally completed and ready to fly, he invited the head of the local tribe to come and watch the event as they started up the plane and it underwent its first test flight.

Everyone gathered on the beach to watch the historic event. Dust, sand and dirt billowed in the air as the Trimotor started up, rolled down the packed sand of the beach and rose into the air. At that point Tom Barger turned to the Bedouin sheikh and said to him in Arabic: "Isn't it wonderful that a machine this big can fly?"

The tribesman replied: "Isn't that what it's supposed to do?"

This gives us some insight into the practical mind of the Saudi desert Bedouin.

One of the early exploration aircraft utilized by CASOC. Photo by Richard Kerr.

---

[2] This aircraft, which arrived in the Kingdom in the late 1930s, was not the company's first. In 1934, CASOC brought in a customized Fairchild 71, adapted for aerial photography, to conduct the first surveys.

Hardy and Barger realized that the Americans and the Saudis needed to utilize the best of each other's way of life. This meant careful recruiting, and emphasis on training and educating individuals who were willing to embrace new concepts, relationships and systems.

Meanwhile, Hardy and Barger began focusing on the wider interests of the Saudi employees – i.e., what was important to them in terms of their families as well as their communities. Tom Barger formed what became known as the "Think Committee," a discussion group made up of mid-level employees whose jobs and experience put them in contact with all nationalities.

The committee was made up primarily of Saudis and other Arabs, and usually included two Americans – of which I was one, and always the more junior member.

Barger would normally be present at the beginning of the meeting to explore and identify issues for discussion, but would then often leave the session to let us deal with those issues free from the scrutiny of senior management. Notes were taken and later given to and discussed with Barger. Harold Beckley, James V. "Jim" Knight, Fred Abbott, Ismail Nazer, Fahmi Basrawi (who usually took notes) and others moved in and out of the Think Committee as subject matter and time permitted.

The committee was not designed to come up with grand, strategic concepts – its discussions highlighted misunderstandings between management and employees and sought to reconcile or resolve the differing expectations of Saudis and Americans and, at times, other foreigners. There were of course many suggestions (similar to what one would find in a suggestion box) but we tried always to steer the discussions toward answering the question "How can we make Aramco a better company and a better place to work?"

Long-range planning discussions were taking place in various departments of the company to find projects that would help Aramco provide necessary infrastructure and improvements for its operations and at the same time assist the Government and the growing communities. For example, Aramco was a major purchaser of a wide variety of supplies, such as packaged foods, farm produce, building materials, automotive equipment, oil field and refining equipment and so on. The towns and villages of the Eastern Province were simply incapable of providing such supplies. Local merchants had never done this sort of mass purchasing and supply for a huge influx of people and projects.

In the early 1940s, Tom Barger compiled a document explaining why the company's very existence in the future would depend on the quality of its relations with the Saudi people and their Government.

Barger was convinced that the people's side of the business would determine its ultimate success or failure. He never abandoned that conviction, and never lost his sensitivity to the aspirations of the Saudis.

Overall, Barger's strategic goal can be summarized in a statement he frequently made: "We are in the business of protecting the concession." To achieve that goal, he truly believed the company had to be as responsive as possible to Saudi Arabia's needs as a fledgling nation with a developing economy.

As I moved up in the organization, I realized that the training and development of the Saudi workforce was not only a long-term economic necessity but also a large part of the formula that would enable Aramco to be recognized as a "good citizen" of the country.

Because of my interest in the Saudi workforce and the aspirations of the Saudi people, I was increasingly drawn into Barger's Think Committee. In those meetings, I usually became the voice of the young technocrat who had a close-up view and understanding of the attitudes of the lower-level workforce – a workforce that was growing by leaps and bounds.

At one point in the mid-1950s, Barger and Cy Hardy decided to set up another committee that would travel to many other oil-producing countries to see at first hand how the petroleum companies in these nations were handling their "good citizenship" problems. Most of these companies were further along in their development than we were, even though they were producing relatively small quantities of oil.

We were particularly interested in community relationships, i.e., how the oil companies interacted with the local workforce, as well as the quality of living facilities for both foreign and local employees. Secondly, we wanted to look at the oil companies' training efforts and their results with their local workforce and, thirdly, we needed to examine the progress of their local contractor and merchant development.

Cy Hardy, with his extensive experience as a Socal executive in South America and elsewhere, took on the chore of obtaining permission to visit oil company operations in countries whose operations were well established and from whom we might obtain useful guidance.

These companies might well be owned by one or more of the Aramco shareholders, some of whom were competitors, not only with each other but also with Aramco. In addition, some of the oil companies were outside competitors of the four Aramco shareholders. Hardy had to convince all of them that our visit would be mutually beneficial.

It was decided that the committee would be made up of Dan Sullivan, a high-ranking Aramco producing executive, A.C.C. "Cliff" Hill, a relations and planning executive, and me. I was probably named the third member because, as a low-level supervisor, I was familiar with the blue-collar and administrative workforce. The three of us went on the road – and into the air – visiting oil companies in a number of producing countries in late 1953 and early 1954.

We received permission and invitations to visit operations in Venezuela, Colombia, Iran, Oman, Bahrain, Kuwait and the Trucial States (which later became the UAE). The Iraq Petroleum Company, owned mostly by French companies, denied our request for a visit.

To put it simply and bluntly, we found that all of these oil operations could best be described as highly colonialist. Some had been in operation quite a bit longer than Aramco. Most had few or no local employees in management positions. Venezuela, which had one operation owned by Exxon and another by Gulf Oil (later acquired by Chevron), had some craft and administrative local employees in mid-management positions, and was trying to integrate them into company-owned areas that housed foreign employees at little or no rent. This integrated rental housing plan was experiencing difficulties of all kinds. Specifically:

- Different schooling was required for English- and Spanish-speaking dependent children.
- Local Venezuelan family units were much larger – they had more children, and elderly relatives lived with the families.
- Similar housing was unavailable in the local towns, so when an employee retired or lost his job, he had to be forced out of his company rental home – which of course produced many problems with his relatives.
- Foreigners and locals had different preferences in food, recreation and after-work facilities.
- Outsiders were gradually encroaching on company facilities – the intermingling of sewage, water and electric systems and heightened security issues created a wide and varying range of management and maintenance

needs. Local Venezuelans, for example, unlike the Americans, had little experience with renting, and consequently had little interest in taking proper care of their rental houses.

In Iran, the differences were similar but magnified, because the local populations near the oil facilities were significantly larger. Local towns, though more populous, still could not accommodate the needs of foreign employees and their families. The Iranian oil facilities were operated by a consortium of companies – a dozen or more. Each foreign oil company would supply management and technical staff to the local company, seconded or assigned on a fee basis, some of them without their families. As loaned employees, they would return to their parent companies after their Iran contracts expired, and thus they gave little or no thought to training or integrating local employees. The loanees, in fact, did minimal long-range thinking about the Iranian oil industry, concentrating instead on getting their day-to-day jobs done over the course of their two-year contracts.

Dissatisfaction among the local employees was already apparent at this early stage, and it surfaced with a vengeance later when ownership, participation and local employee advancement became hot issues in Iran.

Our committee's observations, as gleaned from our travels, led to some significant changes in living accommodations for our employees, especially for the Saudis, who for the most part were being housed on bachelor status. As noted previously, these employees, who usually came from outside our operating areas, were bussed home on weekends if the distance was great, or went home daily if they lived reasonably close to work. Those whose families lived outside the Eastern Province were gradually moving their dependents to the local towns, where they often lived in inferior rental housing with inadequate utilities.

Aramco had already started a Home Ownership Program for Saudi employees, building them good, livable accommodations that they could rent or buy, but this program was meeting with limited success because the houses were designed by foreigners and were in less desirable areas, i.e., they were not located near Aramco operations.

Furthermore, we had seen that oil companies in South America and Iran were having problems renting housing to their local employees. Renters, who generally had little reason to care for and maintain their housing units, were constantly demanding maintenance work, repairs and upgrades. In the eyes of employees, the oil company became the "hated landlord" who cared little about their living requirements.

As spelled out in the 1933 Concession Agreement, Aramco had surface rights to large tracts of land where production might occur. These rights excluded local communities but in most cases ran right up to the city limits of the local towns.

As a result of our global travels, the Home Ownership Program underwent a drastic revision. We began building subdivisions, complete with utilities, adjacent to the local towns, and we transferred the deeds to these plots of land to the employees.

Employees chose their own preferred designs for the homes they wanted to build, and Aramco loaned them the money to build them. Loan payments were deducted from their salaries, and the loans were 16 percent forgiven. This successful program, with some modifications, is still in operation more than 60 years later. It has been shown to be less costly and greatly superior to rental housing, where the company is forced to play the landlord.

Aramco's foreign employees for the most part lived in company compounds that matched their grade-code status. As time went on, some Saudi employees and their families moved into these company quarters when it suited their job requirements. But the overwhelming majority of Saudi employees opted for the Home Ownership Program, becoming owners of their own property at low cost. As a result, new local communities such as Doha and Dana began to develop in neighborhoods adjacent to Dhahran, enriching the economy of the Eastern Province.

Our committee also reviewed such items as pay-scale programs for foreigners versus Saudi nationals, to make sure that they were as equivalent as possible, as well as other employee benefits and work practices. All of this led to continuing revisions in policies aimed at assuring basic fairness for all employees.

An Aramco malarial control specialist examines stagnant water in the Dammam area for mosquito larvae in 1948.

Chapter 9
Healthy and Safe

When the company began to explore for oil in the early days, both American and Saudi employees worked largely in the field, beyond their base camps in Jubail and Dhahran, and very few families lived in company facilities. With the start of crude oil production and associated operations, Aramco faced new responsibilities, among them the major challenge of ensuring the well-being of its new employees and the welfare of their families, who in most cases had journeyed far from home to live in or near company facilities.

Modern medical care was non-existent in Saudi Arabia's eastern area and, indeed, across the Kingdom. Basic emergency treatment could be found at a hospital and small clinics on Bahrain. But American families expected essentially the same level of care they had left behind in the United States. As time went on, by introducing state-of-the-art medical care in Saudi Arabia, Aramco set a high standard for the country and encouraged the development of first-rate medical facilities nationwide.

As the company and the country grew up together, they came to share the same health objectives.

At the beginning, the fresh, new Saudi employees were almost totally unaware of world-class medical care, nor had they previously experienced the kinds of health and safety instruction that the company provided. True, as far as health matters were concerned, these employees were mostly young men with minimal medical needs. Nevertheless, the company mandated that employees – particularly those involved in the hard, physical work of oil operations – receive thorough health and safety training.

As the workforce expanded, advanced and grew older, the employees started their own families, and so awareness grew of the need for adequate healthcare for themselves and their relatives. Saudi employees generally viewed all relatives – children, brothers and sisters, aunts and uncles, grandparents – as part of their extended family.

As more American families began to arrive in 1945-46, a small hospital opened in the central administration community built in Dhahran. Clinics opened in Ras Tanura, our refining and terminal area, and in Abqaiq, our oil production center in the south. These clinics were initially staffed with a doctor, nurses and technicians. Major or complex cases requiring special equipment and surgery were transported to the company's health center in Dhahran. Dental care was also offered at the central facility. Patients with difficult surgical requirements or cases involving specialized and unusual treatment were flown to the United States or Europe.

From about 1947 on, Aramco set in place medical programs to deal with the unique cultural setting and the region's problems of widespread endemic disease, including malaria and trachoma, to ensure that both Saudi and American employees and their families received the same quality medical care.

As the workforce grew, it became necessary to expand the medical program and the Dhahran hospital to the size and scope capable of serving a medium-sized U.S. city. This required staffing commensurate with the needs and standards of such an operation. In the early 1950s, under Dr. Richard H. "Dick" Daggy, director of the Aramco medical department, the hospital was enrolled in a program of the American Commission on Hospital Accreditation (ACHA) that provided regular professional monitoring, inspection and rating of hospitals. Aramco's Dhahran hospital won accreditation and remained fully accredited over the decades to come.

ACHA alone, however, did not provide all the answers to the wide range of medical and health problems facing a pioneering organization in a region lacking familiar infrastructure. From the start, Aramco had to confront the problem of epidemics in local villages, particularly in the oases of Qatif and Safwa, relatively close to the company's base in Dhahran. In addition, many employees and their families lived in and around the city of Hofuf in the sprawling Al-Hasa oasis, south of the Abqaiq production center. Al-Hasa, known for its legendary date-palm orchards, qualified as the world's largest oasis and, along with the Qatif area, became the focus of major efforts to control open water likely to contribute to disease infestation.

Dr. Roger L. Nichols of the Aramco trachoma research team prepares to take an eye scraping from a Saudi Bedouin at a small camp in the desert some 100 miles from Dhahran, October 1957.

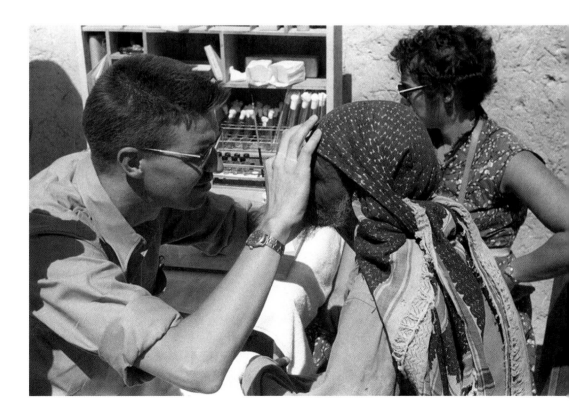

After an initial study, the Aramco medical department moved quickly to introduce preventive measures to control the most prominent and dangerous diseases in the towns and oases of the Eastern Province. Both citizens and local governments needed to be made aware of the efficacy of immunization for preventable diseases such as smallpox, measles, diphtheria, polio and tetanus. The company initiated research programs for such serious threats as malaria, trachoma, sickle cell disease and schistosomiasis (or bilharzia), often with the involvement of local communities.

Although control methods for malaria were well established worldwide, the Saudi public needed training in sanitation and the proper use of water for irrigating the date-palm groves. As new medicines were introduced and the mosquitoes were eliminated through spraying, malaria was brought under control and in time virtually eliminated from the Eastern Province.

Trachoma – a communicable disease of the eyes most prevalent in the developing world and in isolated communities – was rampant in the Gulf region, with many people suffering permanent sight damage and serious eye infections. Trachoma is a bacterial disease, and is spread by human contact, unsanitary conditions and certain insects, such as flies. Aramco hired Dr. Roger Nichols, an American physician, to take the lead in a research effort to control the disease. Nichols had worked at Harvard University on trachoma and similar problems, and he helped develop a joint project between Aramco and Harvard to combat the disease in Saudi Arabia. As a result of this effort, trachoma was virtually eliminated in the Kingdom. The Aramco–Harvard project featured development of proper medication, insect control, improved cleanliness and proper sewage techniques. Trachoma also proved to be a family disease, and was most prevalent in certain families that needed more targeted care. Aramco's trachoma research continued for more than a decade, with the results applied in other countries as well.

Treating Saudi women and their children posed many difficulties because most wives of Saudi employees had never visited a hospital or been treated by trained physicians. They had certainly never been examined by male doctors and were embarrassed and forbidden by custom to be alone in the presence of unknown men. Aramco's hospital staff had to be augmented with Arabic-speaking women who could deal and communicate with female patients, discussing their symptoms and concerns. These visits therefore required longer periods scheduled per patient and consequent sharp increases in medical personnel.

Saudi employees often felt compelled to accompany their families to the hospital and to be present at examinations and treatment visitations. Because their homes were often far away and public transportation was lacking, Saudi employees had to be given as many as two or three days off to escort and transport family members to the hospital and return them to their homes. The time lost was significant, and disrupted work schedules sufficiently to require increased manning.

The answer was to set up small clinics in the local towns, staffed with qualified nurses and medical technicians, who would make the initial contacts with patients, conduct examinations and provide treatment of minor problems such as colds, fevers, superficial wounds and the like. Those with serious problems requiring a doctor's involvement would be scheduled and transported to the hospital in Dhahran.

Dr. Robert E. Oertley of the medical department was credited with doing a creative job in working out the locations and sizes of the staffed local clinics, which were numerous to avoid transportation problems. In addition, a system was put in place to monitor the results in these clinics, to ensure that patients received good medical care and were satisfied with the results. As the clinics became accepted and trusted by Saudi families, employees were more likely to remain at work, greatly reducing the need to increase the workforce to cover excused and unplanned absences for family medical treatment.

At the same time, Aramco's Industrial Development Department teamed up with the Dhahran hospital to encourage the opening of private hospitals and clinics in the Eastern Province that would serve not only the Saudi public but also non-Aramco expatriate labor. Aramco Medical Services, under Dr. A.P. "Phil" Gelpi, inspected these hospitals to ensure high standards of efficiency and cleanliness.

Dentistry presented a somewhat different set of problems. Prior to the creation of Aramco, modern dentistry was virtually non-existent in the area. Dental problems were not treated until an extreme and painful infection occurred, at which point local practitioners invariably extracted the offending teeth by crude, traditional means. This contrasted with the modern dental care that Americans expected and which was more advanced than even the care in Europe. Aramco at first had a small, fully-accredited American dental staff. In those days, very few Saudis or non-American foreign employees called at the dental center unless they desperately needed care. These were patients who showed up with swollen faces and badly-infected teeth.

After experiencing a prompt and relatively painless session with the dentist – which in many cases involved professional extraction – satisfied patients spread the word and appointments for non-Americans rapidly increased. American dentists had to train Indian and later Saudi technicians as quickly as possible to teach patients preventive dental care and to treat minor problems.

As more people were treated, the patient load grew – to the point where dentists would make the initial diagnosis and, if possible, pass the required dental work to skilled technicians, with dentists handling only the more complex, difficult procedures. Because of the workload, treatment was postponed whenever it was not immediately necessary. The non-American patients were amazed and delighted by the treatment they received, but the dentists were disappointed at having to postpone and minimize treatment. Aramco could not supply sufficient qualified dentists in the short term to meet a need that was outgrowing our capability. The answer was more and better technicians to help the dentists and take care of those urgently requiring treatment. In addition, of course, employees and their families had to be taught appropriate personal oral hygiene and care techniques. Aramco did not introduce more specialized dentistry services such as orthodontics for many years, because such services usually had more to do with personal appearance than with oral health.

Aramco's ongoing efforts to improve the health and well-being of its employees quickly found its analogue in the work program, with an emphasis on safety for all employees. The petroleum industry involves heavy equipment, electric power, complex processes and toxic and combustible substances – all involving possible risks to worker safety. High-profile safety programs were initiated in the early 1950s. Safety standards and reporting were introduced throughout the company. Safety reports were made available every day and were discussed with all employees. Improvements in the form of goal-setting and targets were set forth and implemented among employees at all levels, from laborers to high-level management. We organized daily discussions to determine how much progress was being made toward the safety goals we had set, and to explore suggestions for improvements. The company recognized safe performance and the meeting of safety goals by issuing awards, commendations, raises and even promotions.

The Aramco safety record was tabulated by accepted worldwide oil industry and overall industrial standards. By the early 1960s, Aramco's safety record was at the very top of worldwide industrial statistics. It remains so to this day, because safety is now a deeply ingrained, natural way of life for all employees. Senior executives, often led by the CEO, still conduct periodic safety inspections of facilities across Saudi Arabia, organizations and departments have their own customized safety programs, and safety performance remains a serious factor in all employee evaluations.

The early commitment to provide medical care at Aramco soon evolved into a wider challenge as the Saudi Government recognized an overall national need for modern medical treatment for all citizens. Aramco became the model for expanding healthcare across the Kingdom. Aramco's medical department worked hand-in-hand with the Government to plan and implement a quality national health program. Aramco sought to have government and privately-owned facilities take over health programs whenever possible.

We were pleased to see the Government move ahead with a two-pronged approach. It used the Aramco model to set up government clinics and government hospitals in major population centers. At the same time, private investors were encouraged to open small hospitals and clinics that could more quickly provide for local needs – if, of course, they met the highest recognized standards.

In summary, Aramco's record in providing healthcare to employees and dependents, while operating in a harsh environment and a rapidly-changing society, proved to be a satisfying achievement with national implications. It is the story of health services being extended beyond employees and dependents to a needy general public before government services could be widely developed. It is also a story of medical research aimed at eradicating serious diseases, carried out and tailored to the needs of the environment. We were fortunate to witness, and be a part of, an unparalleled example of joint accomplishment and cooperation between a major company and a government over a vast territory and a widely-dispersed society. Keep in mind that the Kingdom's health needs were not only its own, but had also to be expanded dramatically every year to provide medical services during the Hajj – the annual influx of millions of pilgrims from around the world to Islam's Holy Places.

Today the quality of healthcare in Saudi Arabia is recognized as very high, particularly in comparison with other Arab countries. Open-heart surgery and heart transplants, for example, are routine procedures at the Kingdom's top cardiology centers and hospitals. The dramatic growth in Saudi medical expertise is a fact often overlooked by public opinion in the West, which is generally unaware of the strides made by the Saudi monarchy and its high degree of concern for the well-being of its people.

Chapter 10
Trains and Farms:
Lifting an Economy

Over the decade of the 1950s, Aramco accelerated into rapid growth mode. It was hiring, educating and training a new Saudi workforce on an ever-increasing scale. These employees and their large, close-knit families were experiencing a much higher standard of living than ever before. This was national development in action – it was an exciting time for all of us, employees and management alike.

Small merchant businesses in the Kingdom were growing as well, as they sought to supply Aramco's operational, material and service needs wherever and whenever they saw an opening. They also benefited from serving the expanding needs of the booming Aramco employee communities.

The Saudi Government's revenues from Aramco's rising production were also climbing rapidly, just as the needs and desires of some eight to nine million people scattered over this very large country were also being felt.

Widely-dispersed Saudi towns and cities were now calling for improved communications, roads, schools, electricity, water and other infrastructure, as well as imported goods that were hard to find or non-existent in this immense, arid peninsula.

The linking of population centers separated by vast distances required huge expenditure. This had to be done as quickly as possible and on a national scale, to ensure fairness to all regions of the country. This kind of rapid infrastructural expansion needed more revenue than Aramco was currently providing to the Government. To put it bluntly, oil sales were not keeping pace with the Government's spending requirements.

The Government called our attention to this problem as early as 1951, when it became clear that a major bottleneck existed at the port facilities in the Eastern Province. Early on, Aramco had built a small port at Al-Khobar, near Dhahran, to receive cargo from the sailing dhows, which were transshipping imported goods offloaded from freighters at a large port in Bahrain, about 15 miles away.

By the mid-1940s, a slightly larger port with deeper water access had opened at Dammam, north of Al-Khobar, and cargo ships were then able to bypass Bahrain and offload directly in Saudi Arabia. More goods began to arrive at Dammam, destined not only for Aramco but also for the fast-growing capital city of Riyadh. At this point, shipping freight onward from the port of Dammam became a problem as well.

Aramco had built a short railroad from Dammam port to Dhahran and a network of roads within the Aramco area of operations to handle the movement of its own imports of oilfield construction equipment and other freight. But the shipments destined for Riyadh were often stuck in the port, due to a lack of adequate transportation to the capital. The roads to Riyadh were barely passable and trucks – in short supply to begin with – had to travel more than 350 miles to deliver cargo to the capital. The Government at this time had neither the funds nor the resources to resolve the problem in short order. So, after negotiations with the Government, Aramco agreed to provide a solution by building a larger, deep-water port facility about seven miles offshore at Dammam, along with docking facilities and a railroad line that ran from the port all the way to the capital.

A Saudi Government railroad train arrives in Dammam in December 1955.

Aramco engaged Bechtel Corp. to design, engineer and later build the railroad. After completion, Aramco initially staffed the port and the railroad and operated both until 1952, when they were sold to the Government as properly-financed operating businesses. These facilities were expanded and continually improved over time by the Government. The deep-water facility at Dammam, called King Abdulaziz Port, is one of nine major port facilities now operated by the Saudi Ports Authority. The Dammam–Riyadh rail line is now owned by the Saudi Railways Organization, which has continued to improve the system, and plans to extend its rail network to Jeddah on the west coast and eventually north to Jordan and south to Yemen. In other words, the port and rail system begun by Aramco is thriving today as a primary export-import lifeline and an example of how Aramco and the Government worked together to meet a sharply-growing material need.

Growing the Food Supply

Another logistical problem needed prompt resolution – providing a regular food supply to the burgeoning Aramco employee and contractor workforce. Growing numbers of Western – mostly American – engineers and technicians and their families were taking up residence in the Aramco communities, along with the steady influx of Saudis and their families, not only from the Eastern Province but also from the western and central parts of the Kingdom. These rapid changes demanded logistical solutions that would serve not only the company's needs but also those of the entire nation of Saudi Arabia.

The convergence of large numbers of Aramco families meant the company needed to import foodstuffs, medical supplies, housing materials and the like which were not yet available locally.

Local fruits and vegetables are loaded on trucks destined for markets in the Eastern Province, 1954.

The Saudi diet consisted primarily of lamb, rice, dates and a few vegetables. These foods were primarily grown in two major eastern oases (Al-Hasa and Al-Qatif) and one government-owned facility at Al-Kharj, southeast of Riyadh. In the oases, artesian wells were used to provide water for the date orchards and livestock, in those days almost exclusively sheep and goats. The agricultural production of these two oases was constrained by limited water availability. The Al-Kharj project used water pumped from a large underground aquifer.

Aramco needed to expand the production of foodstuffs and produce – eggs, meat, fruit and vegetables of all kinds. At first, Aramco imported virtually all its meat from Australia, since it was closer to Saudi Arabia than was the U.S.. However the food preferences of Aramco westerners were different from those of Australians. Meat cuts provide an example: Australian suppliers had to be instructed as to which cuts of beef met the requirements of the Americans and which cuts of lamb met the needs of the Saudis – both types of cut being different from those preferred in the Australian market.

Lamb and beef were the primary meats imported initially, along with chicken, which came from the United States. Domestic supplies of chicken meat and eggs were rather modest at first, but they quickly became a priority as demand increased among the Saudi workforce. Local chicken farms were quickly introduced and encouraged by Aramco.

A separate agricultural assistance division was set up as part of Aramco's Arab Industrial Development Department (AIDD) to encourage oasis farmers to grow vegetables and fruit. Sometimes the suggestions fell on deaf ears. Aramco proposed that Saudi farmers grow carrots, but these root vegetables were not part of the local diet at the time and farmers could not imagine that there would be a market for them. AIDD found ways to sweeten the deal and encourage the growth of carrots, which eventually became popular with Saudis. The company not only furnished seeds but also gave farmers guidance in carrot-growing techniques and the appropriate use of fertilizer.

Steps were also taken to remove salt deposits that had accumulated over many years in the soil of the farming oases. The salt resulted from the overuse of oasis artesian water, which generally had a higher salt content. One of the main techniques was to flood the fields with sweet water and leach the salt from the soil. At first the farmers saw this method as a waste of precious drinking water, until they realized that harvests increased as the salt was removed.

These ideas and others helped bring about greater agricultural yields. In the case of carrots, the farmers were still reluctant to grow them until Aramco promised to purchase the crops. With that guarantee, farmers started planting large quantities of carrot crops. They were slow to make room for other types of vegetables until they could count on the Aramco market. In time, the Saudi public began buying and enjoying crops originally intended for Aramco – one by one, a wide variety of new fruit and vegetables began to enrich the national diet.

Aramco's agricultural assistance division grew rapidly and served as an important forerunner of what became a significant national farm production industry. Under the guidance of the Ministry of Agriculture, the Saudi farming industry improved over the years to the point that today the Kingdom exports a considerable amount of its farm produce. The Government paved the way for a national farming industry in the early 1940s, when it launched an agricultural program in Central Arabia aimed at feeding the residents of the greater Riyadh area. That was when Al-Kharj, with its available groundwater and fertile soil, was opened up to farming.

'Abd Allah Al-Matrood worked for Aramco in the 1930s and 1940s as a laundry man, collecting the soiled clothes of Aramco employees and taking them to Bahrain for cleaning, as there were no local laundries at the time. After the war, the company encouraged him to form his own business, National Laundry. He later started his own dairy company, National Dairy and Ice Cream Plant.

Al-Matrood's dairy operation is one of about eight local companies producing milk, butter, yogurt and cheese for the domestic market. These companies now account for almost all the fresh, pasteurized milk sales in Saudi Arabia, 90 percent of the domestic market for *laban* (a traditional Middle Eastern drink similar to natural drinking yogurt) and 94 percent of the Saudi market for yogurt.[1] As a result of efforts by these firms and the Saudi farmers who supply them, the Kingdom has become almost self-sufficient in dairy products and is exporting these foodstuffs to a number of neighboring Gulf countries.

The steadily-expanding market that Aramco provided was a powerful incentive for Saudi entrepreneurs willing to take risks. Food supply was only part of a much

---

[1] M.M. Al-Otaibi and R.K. Robinson, "The Dairy Industry in Saudi Arabia: Current Situation and Future Prospects," *International Journal of Dairy Technology*, Vol. 55, No. 2, May 2002.

larger picture. Some key businesses, such as a pipe-coating plant and an oxygen and acetylene plant, were started on the basis of purchase contracts from Aramco, which made it possible for entrepreneurs to obtain financing. In other instances, the company guaranteed loans or provided other financing to assist local business ventures. In most cases, Aramco waited for a local businessman to establish a company and demonstrate its capabilities before winding down its equivalent operation and shifting the business to the local provider.

By the mid-1950s, Aramco was paying some $12 million a year to local contractors for goods and services. In 1956, these local firms were employing at least 3,000 Saudi nationals. The numbers have grown steadily ever since.

As the domestic economy grew, many individuals who got their start at Aramco went on to create successful local businesses that sometimes became national and even international enterprises. One such success story involved a Saudi named Suliman Olayan. One of the very earliest CASOC and Aramco employees (his badge number was 40!), Olayan listened when Aramco began encouraging Saudis to start their own businesses and become contractors for the company.

Olayan had started as a transportation dispatcher for CASOC and rose to a respected position in Aramco Government Relations. In 1947, he left his job at Aramco and opened a trucking company in Al-Khobar. His company handled transportation for Bechtel, then under contract to build the huge Tapline oil pipeline system across northern Saudi Arabia.[2] By 1954, Olayan started another company that handled the trucking of foodstuffs to Aramco communities. In time, Olayan became one of the world's most successful and wealthiest businessmen, overseeing the operations of The Olayan Group, a huge business enterprise of global scope.

Olayan was one of the earliest Saudi employees to become a local business success, but over the years there were many others who were also very important to

_____

[2] The Trans-Arabian Pipeline Company (Tapline) operated an oil pipeline that extended from the Eastern Province of Saudi Arabia to a tanker terminal at Sidon, Lebanon. Originally founded as a separate joint venture of the four American partners, it eventually became a wholly-owned subsidiary of Aramco. Local communities grew up around the pumping stations, at locations such as Qaisumah and Badanah. The pipeline itself has not been used for decades and the subsidiary that operated it was shut down in 2002.

the Saudi economy – who took Aramco's advice, launched businesses of their own, and helped drive their country's economic miracle.

Former Aramco employee 'Ali Al-Tamimi turned his Dammam Laundry of the 1950s into a multifaceted enterprise that included construction services, transportation and supermarkets. 'Abd Allah Fouad left the company in the late 1940s to provide various support services to Aramco, and in 1962 formed a partnership with Al-Tamimi that moved from pipeline contracting to a wide range of local businesses. (Fouad and Al-Tamimi, incidentally, made substantial contributions to Saudi society by helping to fund and build hospitals and other medical facilities in the Eastern Province.) Other families that moved from employment with Aramco, or providing services to Aramco, to national business prominence – giving back to Saudi society along the way – include the Zamils (Zamil Group), the Rushaids (Al-Rushaid Group), the Algosaibis (Hamad Algosaibi & Bros.), the Al-Gahtanis (HAK Group) and many others.

Not only was the company growing apace, but also local businesses were expanding along with it, benefiting from Aramco's presence and the commercial launching pad it provided for Saudi entrepreneurs.

Chapter 11
Interlude at Shemlan

In 1962, I was encouraged by Aramco to spend a year in Arabic language training at an appropriate school or university. I received advice on this from knowledgeable staff in our Employee Relations Department, as well as personal input from CEO Tom Barger, who was something of an Arabist and knew the language well. As a result of these conversations, I decided to take advantage of the best study opportunities located in the Middle East itself, where I could be immersed in an Arabic-speaking society in addition to benefiting from the language program.

I selected the Middle East Center for Arabic Studies (MECAS) in Lebanon for a number of reasons, but primarily because it had a good track record of teaching Arabic and Arab culture to English-speaking students. The British Government had opened MECAS in 1947. Over the years, it gained a reputation among the general public – often jokingly – as "the British spy school," not only because young diplomats studied there but also because George Blake, a British double agent who spied on behalf of the Soviet Union had been a student there. MECAS was closed down in 1978 because of the Lebanese Civil War. Today its buildings house an orphanage for mentally handicapped children.

The British Foreign Office operated MECAS in the small village of Shemlan, on a high cliff that boasted a spectacular view of the Lebanese capital to the west. The 50-mile drive from Beirut took about an hour and a half on a winding highway that continued on to the Roman ruins at Baalbek and then across the Syrian border to Damascus.

Shemlan was somewhat secluded, on an unpaved road a few miles south of the highway. The sleepy little village was located in the Shuf, historically a Druze stronghold, but by now Shemlan had become home to mostly Maronite Christians, with a few Druze leaders as a reminder of the community's history. This was the home village of Philip Hitti, the famous Middle East historian of Princeton University.

The MECAS complex at Shemlan featured classrooms, individual bedrooms, library and dining facilities staffed by local Lebanese. The instructors were from

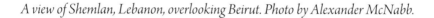

A view of Shemlan, Lebanon, overlooking Beirut. Photo by Alexander McNabb.

varied Arab backgrounds, mostly Palestinians, whose Arabic was regarded as somewhat less flavored with dialect than, say, Lebanese, Syrian or Egyptian.

The student capacity was about 30 – predominantly British Foreign Office employees, fresh graduates of Oxford and Cambridge destined to be stationed at embassies and consulates in the Arab world. I was one of only three American students assigned for this particular school year, and as such we were exposed to British educational methods rarely encountered in the United States. All weekly test scores were publicly posted, and students were assigned to one of ten three-man syndicates, ranked in order of its students' progress to date. Thus the three highest-ranking students, based on grades, in the first syndicate were moved through the curriculum more rapidly than those in lower-ranking syndicates. This further accelerated those individuals and their individual progress until they were overtaken by someone below them who had worked all the harder. It was a very effective treadmill, with all results posted regularly on the bulletin board.

Another major indicator of progress was the speed with which we learned new words. Students were presented with a 10,000-word list divided by 50 weeks per year, or 200 words per week, and arranged roughly by listing the most used nouns and verbs first. We had to make up some 30 flash cards every day, with Arabic words on one side and English on the other, and then flip through the cards, speaking the words aloud in both languages. The student could ask for a test whenever he felt he had mastered 400 words, and if he passed, he moved on to the next list.

Memorizing a word list meant reviewing each previous daily list in the 400-word group, and adding 30 new words, while still retaining the past items in your memory, until you felt confident you could pass the next test.

Shuffling stacks of flash cards each day was a grim drudgery that could only be relieved by taking a weekend trip to Beirut – in my case, to join my wife and two sons, who were living there while I undertook my language studies. Beirut in those years was a thriving, bustling, beautiful city of multiple religions, different types of Arabs, many languages, and a beautiful Mediterranean Sea coastline. In my opinion, and for many others as well, Beirut ranked as one of the top three cities to be visited anywhere in the world – along with London and San Francisco.

On one of these weekend trips down the mountain to the city, I was driving my own American car, which was really too big for the streets and roads at that time. Jim Knight, an American classmate from Aramco, sat beside me, along with three

British students in the back seat. All of us were glad to be out of Shemlan for a couple of days, and I remarked to Knight that one problem with this full year of studies was that when we finished school, we would be speaking Arabic like a Lebanese and English like a Brit – to which one of the British classmates behind us piped up: "An improvement, I dare say!"

Back at school, I had established a routine of going every morning for breakfast at a small restaurant run by the *mukhtar* or mayor of the village. The place was little more than a grapevine-sheltered patio from which you could look down on the sprawling city of Beirut, lit by morning sunlight. The first day I went there, I asked the mayor in my beginner's Arabic if I could get a couple of eggs and some bread, and then added: "Are the eggs fresh?" Within a few minutes, one of his granddaughters came running to my table with an egg in each hand. She put the eggs against my cheeks. They were still warm, having just been laid. From that morning on, every time I came to breakfast, the little girl came running with fresh, warm eggs as I busily flipped through my flash cards.

After our classroom studies had been completed, we were tested on oral and written translation skills, to determine our graduating score. In addition, we were required to take a local job for about six weeks that would give us a chance to use Arabic on a daily basis. After six weeks, we would return to MECAS and be retested to see what impact daily Arabic usage had on our final test score.

I took a job teaching English and basic arithmetic to Arabic-speaking Palestinian students in about the seventh or eighth grade – or maybe a little younger – in a United Nations refugee camp south of Sidon. These boys were eager to learn anything I could teach them, but they were part of a bitter generation, caught up like many since then in complete dismay and despair over their statelessness and resentment at having been driven from their homeland. Every morning, the boys would stand outside the classroom with arms extended, swearing they would take back their country when they grew older. They would question me a lot about my views on their situation. I had my car there, and in the evening I would load up some of the boys and we would head into downtown Sidon to get some dinner – something tastier and more substantial than the bare minimum they were receiving in the understaffed and underfinanced refugee camps. When I ate breakfast with them in the camp – usually one egg and a piece of hard bread – one of the boys once asked: "What do you think of this breakfast?" Of course it was a loaded question for me, the distrusted

American. But I learned to answer questions like this. In this case I simply said: "Look, you know that I take you out to dinner – as many of you as I can – in the evenings. So you know I understand the difference between meals here and there. I have to admit that, for me, this breakfast is pretty minimal. But for you, it's the best you can expect from the United Nations under the circumstances. What more can I say? This is the truth of the matter." The boys seemed satisfied with my answer. In this way, I managed to establish myself as a realist who was trying to help.

My return to Shemlan for final testing did produce a significant improvement in my spoken Arabic and thus my graduating grade.

I should note that this was not the last time during my years in the Middle East that I had to field difficult and controversial questions from Palestinians. I learned to respond by stating the facts, if possible with a bit of humor.

In late 1969 and early 1970, I was in charge of Aramco's Concession Affairs organization, which included Public Relations. In those days, Lebanon's capital city, with its vibrant press and multicultural outlook, was the place to discuss weighty issues of politics and policy. I decided to visit Beirut every three months or so if possible, to meet with Lebanese and Syrian businessmen, academics and politicians to discuss world affairs, the economy and Aramco's needs and activities. I wanted to improve ties with Arab leaders there, who generally felt Aramco should be more active in informing Americans about the plight of the Palestinian people.

These meetings, whether large or small, were generally quite useful and took place in a cordial atmosphere. The head of our Beirut office, Shafiq W. Kombargi, a Lebanese of Palestinian background, would usually set up these get-togethers in the context of a small luncheon. At one meeting, however, the attendance became quite large, so we held the luncheon outside on a typically beautiful sunny Beirut day, with many small tables and a congenial atmosphere all round. The luncheon was attended by a number of well-known Palestinian leaders, including Yassir Arafat of Fatah and Dr. George Habash of the Popular Front for the Liberation of Palestine (PFLP).

After lunch, I said a few words about how things were going in our business and related some news about our commercial activities in Lebanon. I noted that a significant number of American high school students were studying at the American Community School in Beirut and that students of all nationalities were being trained and educated at the American University of Beirut (AUB). Of course, Aramco and its subsidiary Tapline had considerable purchasing and business interests in Lebanon as well.

As I finished my remarks, Dr. Habash asked to speak. He said he knew that Aramco tried to be helpful and had a substantial commercial impact in Saudi Arabia and the Levant, but he contended that the company had done little to alleviate the plight of the Palestinians because of the Israeli bias in the U.S. Congress. He rambled on at great length, saying in effect: "The U.S. Senate is small – only 100 people – while Aramco is a huge, wealthy company. We all know that politicians can be bought. So why don't you just buy the senators?"

The gathering erupted in loud cheers and jeers, after which the Arab guests waited for my answer. I replied: "I have given a lot of thought to this problem, usually without reaching a satisfactory conclusion. So I guess I can only say: Yes, there are 100 senators, and you here today are fewer than 100 – perhaps I should buy you."

The noise and jeers that followed quickly dissolved into laughter and applause, as the futility of the question became apparent. We then ordered tea.

Chapter 12
The Faisal Era Begins

During the mid-1960s, the oil-producing countries of the world grew increasingly critical of their concessionary companies for not preferentially lifting more petroleum to generate more revenue for national development. The post-war developing world was seething with change, as nations became independent or developed awareness of their potential, and pursued Western, Eastern or hybrid models of modernization. Most of the countries needed increasing sums of money for infrastructural development as demanded by their populations. This reality engendered competition between nations, because a dozen or more major companies held partial oil industry ownership in multiple countries. Developing countries began talking about nationalizing the concessionary companies.

In Saudi Arabia, Abdullah H. Al-Tariki, the Kingdom's first Minister of Petroleum, was definitely becoming more vocal in his demands for greater responsiveness from

Aramco during the years of King Saud's reign (1953-64). When Saud's half-brother Faisal became King in 1964, Sheikh Ahmed Zaki Yamani had already replaced Al-Tariki as Petroleum Minister (at then-Crown Prince Faisal's request).

The colorful Sheikh Yamani first became an advisor to the Saudi Government in 1958 and was the Minister of Petroleum and Mineral Resources from 1962 to 1986, representing the Kingdom in OPEC, the Organization of Petroleum Exporting Countries, for 25 years. He has academic degrees from New York University School of Law and Harvard Law School. After his years in government, he founded the London-based Centre for Global Energy Studies in 1990, and he has received honorary doctorates from several leading universities around the world.

At the beginning of King Faisal's reign, Yamani realized that the global oil market was weak – prices were down due to surplus supplies in the market, global inflation and a weaker U.S. dollar – and he let this be known in Saudi Arabia, arguing that a better tactic might be to think in terms of taking part-ownership in Aramco rather than pursuing nationalization as some other countries were doing. He introduced the term "participation" for this concept.

King Faisal ibn Abdulaziz. Photo courtesy of Hulton-Deutsch Collection/Corbis.

Aramco's four shareholders were grappling with the weak oil market, which was cutting into their earnings. The Aramco Board pressed company management to explain clearly to the Saudi Government that this worldwide marketing problem was exacerbated by the fact that crude oil types and qualities varied from country to country. Quality differences and varying prices also meant different levels of earnings for the producing countries.

The senior vice president of Concession Affairs, Robert I. Brougham[1] – and later myself, when I was assigned to this position – would scrupulously inform our shareholders by coded cable of any discussions we might hold with the Saudi Government on this complex subject. The four partners would then provide us with their carefully considered thoughts and suggestions – also via coded wireless, since telephone communications with the Middle East were at the time very unreliable and frequently monitored.

We had a secure communications room in the basement of our main headquarters building in Dhahran that was manned 24 hours a day, 7 days a week, with fully-qualified American technicians. It housed the latest in telex equipment, which could send and receive coded communications to and from our New York office. New York would in turn relay messages to our shareholder directors. We also had high-frequency (HF) radio equipment for voice communications with the New York office and with our aircraft when weather conditions permitted. HF radio transmission at that time was not secure.

Aramco had its own telephone system in Saudi Arabia, encompassing office and home service in our communities and operating facilities. This system was tied into the Saudi national communications system in the early 1980s, when technological advances blossomed worldwide.

But back in the 1960s and early 1970s, reliable and secure voice communications were not available throughout most of the Middle East. The closest facilities that met such requirements could be found in Greece, and from time to time we would need to fly to Athens, some four hours away, to conduct confidential voice communications. Hotels in Athens with adequate phone service were still considerably less than five-star accommodations, and it was relatively difficult to rent adequate rooms outside

---

[1] Robert Brougham served as chairman and CEO of Aramco in 1969–70.

Aramco's Board of Directors holds one of its meetings at the site of Dammam Well No. 7 in Dhahran, in October 1962. At the center is Chairman Thomas Barger. Fourth from left, in his first year on the Board, is Sheikh Ahmed Zaki Yamani.

of hotels from which to make our calls – most of these were not secure either. To make matters worse, the working week in the Middle East began on Saturday and ended on Wednesday. This left Monday, Tuesday and Wednesday as the only days that coincided with the U.S. working week – not to mention the eight-hour time difference with New York, home of three of the Aramco partners, and the 11-hour difference with San Francisco, where Socal was based.

The great distances involved and the poor state of telecommunications in the Middle East also affected Western news coverage of the region. There were few Western journalists based in Saudi Arabia. Even as late as the 1970s, when it came to covering news from the Kingdom, Western wire services like AP, UPI and Reuters plus a handful of major newspapers had to rely on stringer-correspondents or freelancers in Jeddah or Riyadh, who usually held down full-time jobs with local English-language newspapers like *Arab News* (founded in 1975) or *Saudi Gazette* (1976). There were no Kingdom-based staff correspondents for the American or European television or radio networks. The world press often lacked reliable knowledge of what was going on inside Saudi Arabia and other less-covered countries of the Middle East. The international press would sometimes produce bizarre news articles about such countries. The French press in those days seemed to rely on the Israeli news media for much of its coverage of the region, and thus sometimes relayed what amounted to very biased reports on evnts in Arab lands.

King Faisal was very wary of the press in general and had no confidence in the European press, especially the French – as a result, international journalists were often barred from visiting the Kingdom. We knew that King Faisal rarely allowed himself to be interviewed.

In the early 1970s, during a series of difficult negotiations between Aramco and the Saudi Government, an article appeared in the Israeli press and was conveyed to the rest of the world by the French media, claiming that I personally was having problems with the Government of Saudi Arabia. Supposedly I was being uncooperative with King Faisal's suggestion that the Saudi Government be given oil to market on its own. This story was utter, unfounded nonsense. Aramco routinely provided oil to Saudi Arabia to meet domestic needs on a normal commercial basis. Furthermore, any special requests from the Saudi Government or the King were answered and dealt with promptly and equitably.

However, the press continued to generate articles spreading this specious claim. Apparently, some in France and Israel were working to develop a myth about the "imperialistic oil company" (Aramco) seeking to control Saudi Arabia, posing problems for the cause of Israel, and so forth.

The rumor about my "uncooperativeness" persisted, seemingly being fed by unknown outside sources. It moved from being a laughing matter to a real concern. Once, when I was outside the Kingdom on business, an article appeared in the press reporting that I had been expelled from Saudi Arabia. When I returned on schedule – and of course had no re-entry problems – I drove from the Dhahran airport to my home to find Saudi plainclothes secret police in my yard.

I asked the man in charge: "What are you doing here?"

He said: "Looking for Palestinians. Some are threatening oil companies, for terrorist reasons. We will remain here until they are apprehended."

After a few days, the government security men withdrew and things seemed to return to normal – until one morning my secretary, Mary Frances Rose, an American woman who had worked in Saudi Arabia for many years, got a call from the Royal Protocol Office in Riyadh.

She told me: "The Protocol Office called, saying they wondered why we had been delinquent in not paying a courtesy call on the King."

We normally made such courtesy calls on a regular basis, and she thought that we were about on schedule. Nonetheless, I asked her to promptly make an appointment for a few days later, knowing that we would normally be granted an audience unless the King was out of the country. Our request for an appointment received the response "two weeks or so," which was unusually vague and quite unlike his normal office schedule.

On the appointed day, I went to see the King, taking along Majed A. Elass – a Syrian-born, American-educated Aramco executive – as an advisor/interpreter, because I wanted to be certain to understand the King accurately, given the growing complexity of this press controversy. When we arrived, we did not meet the King in his office, as we usually did, but were sent instead to a large meeting room. We waited there alone for quite a while. Eventually King Faisal came in, sat down and ordered tea for us. He seemed uneasy and began plucking at the hairs of his camelhair robe, a mannerism that usually indicated he was irritated about something.

He was not talkative and I had no specific agenda, so I tried to pass the time with pleasantries, which had little or no helpful effect. I had learned long before that one difference between Saudis and Americans is that when sitting together, we Americans always feel compelled to fill the silences with small talk. However, when just sitting and waiting with a Saudi companion, if you have nothing to say – don't say it. In an Arab social environment, it's not necessary to keep talking. So on this morning with the King, we just sat and waited for what seemed a long time and he seemed to grow increasingly ill at ease.

Finally the door burst open and in came the press, mostly French photographers and news cameramen. They began taking pictures – it was a photo opportunity or "photo op," which for King Faisal was unprecedented. They took close-ups of the King and me from all angles. Finally His Majesty had had enough, and motioned for them to leave the room. They hurriedly picked up their gear and departed. The King then called for coffee and tea, and suddenly he became quite cordial.

We talked about various matters for some time. Eventually, he said he was busy and we parted with smiles. During our conversation, it dawned on me that the photo op had been King Faisal's way of defusing the media controversy over the Aramco–Government relationship. If he had called me in and told me not to worry about the French and Israeli press, I might wonder why that was necessary. But the King had figured out a way to tell me clearly and most definitely that there was no problem with me or with Aramco as far as he was concerned, and that I should understand that. Any denial he might have made to the press would have only raised more questions.

Majed A. Elass, left, and Frank Jungers, right, congratulate Abdelaziz Shalfan, Badge No. 4, on achieving forty years of service with Aramco.

Photos of us together, taken by French photographers, would deal with that problem. There was no need to say anything more about a news story that had no basis in fact in the first place.

King Faisal was known for his masterful personal and political skills, which made him so popular and fondly remembered by the Saudi people. This incident showed the master at his best.

Chapter 13
Bahrain and the Abu Sa'fah Field

In 1963, Aramco announced discovery of oil in an offshore field in the shallow Gulf waters between the Saudi Arabia's east coast and nearby Bahrain Island (then still a British Protectorate). The field was named Abu Sa'fah.

The island nation of Bahrain is actually an archipelago of some three dozen islands. The four largest islands – including the main one, Bahrain Island itself – are connected by bridges and make up a landmass about four times the size of the District of Columbia. Bahrain's capital city is Manama. The country has a long and rich archaeological history, and ancient ruins of the storied civilization of Dilmun, a trading partner of Sumeria in the fourth millennium BC, have been discovered and identified there.

Before modern times, Bahrain was famous for its pearling industry. Its oyster beds produced relatively large high-quality pearls that were harvested by skilled divers using traditional dhows. Fishing was also a good local industry. In 1932, Socal's Bahrain Petroleum Company (Bapco) discovered oil on the main island. The field was of modest size and its initial production soon declined, requiring pressure maintenance techniques to maintain good production levels. The company built a pier to load tankers and later a small refinery was added.

As noted previously, geologists working in Bahrain were the first to realize the significance of a large rock dome structure across the water in Saudi Arabia that suggested the presence of substantial oil reserves. It was this structure – the Dammam Dome – that helped convince Socal to seek a concession agreement with the relatively new Saudi Government. By the early 1940s, after Socal's CASOC had discovered oil in the Kingdom and was producing it for export, an underwater pipeline was built to ship Saudi crude oil to Bapco facilities in Bahrain. Thus, from the very beginning, the company that would later be known as Aramco had solid relations with Bahrain and its own oil company Bapco.

In time, commercial airlines began flying into Bahrain and Aramco employees frequented the island, which offered some Western-style amenities. Manama featured expanded shopping options and various kinds of entertainment – movie theaters, trendy restaurants and the like – that did not exist in Saudi Arabia.

Fees from underwater pipelines for shipping Aramco crude through their terminal for export, along with revenues from Bahrain's own small oilfields, supported the Bahraini government and the basic needs of the people, who were and still are predominantly Shi'ite Muslims. By contrast, the Bahraini ruling family, which had been in power for more than a century, was Sunni.

In centuries past, the nearby kingdom of Persia, now Iran, had occupied these islands. The Persians (or Iranians) were Shi'ite and of Aryan ethnic stock. Iranians are not Semitic Arabs and they speak a different language (Farsi), which happens to use the Arabic script and alphabet. The Iranians finally lost control of Bahrain in about 1783, when their Arab clients were defeated in battle by the Arabian Bani 'Utbah tribe of Najd, which had in fact had a presence on the islands dating back to the 17th century. Since then, at various times Iran has voiced claims to the islands, based on their historical presence there – claims that have been rejected by the Bahrainis and, of course, by Saudi Arabia.

The Arab–Persian rivalry in the Gulf manifested itself in the media in the early 1950s, when Saudi Arabia launched public efforts to discontinue the use of the term "Persian Gulf" and insisted that all maps, publications and books change that name to "Arabian Gulf." Over time, new publications and references in the Arab countries of the region have almost completely discontinued the use of the term "Persian Gulf."

The relationship between the Saudis and Bahrainis has always been very cordial and marked by cooperation, even though culturally and socially Bahrain has been more liberal and despite the large Shi'ite population there.

From its earliest days, Aramco employed Bahraini labor, and people moved freely between the two countries, mostly by boat. In the 1980s, to make travel easier and to demonstrate Saudi Arabia's commitment to Bahrain in the face of Iranian saber-rattling, the Saudis built a 14-mile multi-lane causeway to Bahrain. The causeway also served as a kind of "relief valve" for those Saudis and their families who wanted to spend a weekend or so enjoying the international flavor of shopping and entertainment in Bahrain.

In the early 1960s, Bahrain's government saw that infrastructural development and improved services were becoming necessary to keep up with regional standards and encourage visitors from Saudi Arabia and other countries. The Bahrainis realized that they needed more revenue than their own oil development could supply. When Aramco delineated the new offshore oilfield called Abu Sa'fah in 1963, the Bahrainis were delighted to learn that they would be receiving an equal share of the revenue from the field, despite the fact that it lay completely on the Saudi side of the offshore boundary between the two countries. This was because, in 1958, Saudi Arabia and Bahrain had reached an offshore boundary agreement that gave Bahrain 50 percent of the net income resulting from exploration for oil resources lying in the area of Abu Sa'fah Reef on the Saudi side of the delineated boundary line. Saudi Arabia viewed this as a gesture of support for the friendly government of Bahrain.

Bahrain readily agreed that Aramco should operate the field and that the government in Manama would receive a pro-rata share of the Abu Sa'fah production revenue.

Abu Sa'fah was somewhat more complex to operate and thus more costly to produce at higher rates than the average Aramco field. Operating management selected an optimum rate and so informed the Bahraini government.

Sometime later, Aramco received a call from Saudi Petroleum Minister Yamani's office: King Faisal wanted to see us regarding production from Abu Sa'fah. When we met, the King told me that the Bahraini ruler had called him and asked for an increase in Abu Sa'fah production, because his government needed more revenue to meet the country's budgetary requirements. I explained to King Faisal why we were producing at the current rates, which were most economical for Aramco and the Kingdom. He replied that, regardless of profitability, he really wanted us to produce the field at a higher rate, if at all possible. He asked Aramco to do this favor for the Bahrainis. The King said it was embarrassing not to be doing more for them, and the Bahrainis too were embarrassed to be asking favors of Saudi Arabia. He asked us to work this out at the oilfield operating level and not as a high-level government-to-government negotiation. He did not want to make an international issue out of the Bahraini request. I was obviously being asked to adjust production to generate more earnings under the existing formula. The formula itself was not to be a subject of discussion.

I asked if the Saudi Government would set up a date for us to meet with the Bahrainis. The King replied that I should make my own arrangements, so it would not be construed as an official meeting. He said the Bahrainis would be expecting my call. So we set a date to travel to Bahrain to meet with the Emir, Sheikh Isa bin Salman Al Khalifa, and his Minister of Development, Yousuf Al-Shirawi.[1]

Sheikh Isa and I had met before. He was very short in stature, with a perpetual, likable grin and a positive outlook. He was quite active in the country, constantly interacting with his people, and he made special efforts to meet with foreigners and make them feel welcome.

We talked about the revenue problem, and the Emir and his Minister sincerely hoped we would do our best to help, since Bahrain at that time received about 50 percent of its governmental revenues from Abu Sa'fah. He asked me to sit with Yousuf Al-Shirawi and the Minister of Finance to work something out. He did not want to put undue pressure on us, but certainly hoped we could be helpful. The Emir left early. After a long discussion with the two ministers, I asked them to tell me the size of the deficit and I showed them the problems we had with the production of the oilfield. We finally reached a long-term solution whereby we would meet annually at budget time to chart the year ahead. An Aramco financial executive would meet with them to discuss their revenue requirements and the precise timing of payments. Aramco would then make a best effort to meet the Bahraini requirements using the pro-rata rates that were in place.

I went back to Saudi Arabia and reported the agreed solution to King Faisal, who asked his Minister of Finance, Mohammed A. Abalkhail, to oversee what they viewed as a good solution to the problem.

The bottom line – Aramco was able to produce a realistic solution to an international problem without resorting to awkward renegotiation.

----

[1] Sheikh Isa ruled as Emir of Bahrain from 1961 to 1999. Upon his death, he was succeeded by his son, Sheikh Hamad bin Isa Al Khalifah, who declared himself King in 2002.

Chapter 14
Boundaries

Aramco's original concession from the Kingdom of Saudi Arabia encompassed some 381,000 square miles (988,000 square kilometers.) of land, located exclusively in the eastern half of the Arabian Peninsula.

The Concession Agreement required the company to relinquish certain amounts of land by specified dates.[1] Aramco could relinquish any areas it wished

---

[1] Article 9 of the original Concession Agreement (May 29, 1933): "Within ninety days after the commencement of drilling, the Company shall relinquish to the Government such portions of the exclusive area as the Company at that time may decide not to explore further, or to use otherwise in connection with this enterprise. Similarly, from time to time during the life of this contract, the Company shall relinquish to the Government such further portions of the exclusive area as the Company may then decide not to explore or prospect further, or to use otherwise in connection with the enterprise. The portions so relinquished shall thereupon be released from the terms and conditions

from the concession, provided they met the area requirements and were turned back to the Saudi Government by the agreed dates. The accord also gave Aramco preferential rights in an area in Central Arabia, with terms to be agreed. Therefore, over time, a number of negotiations took place that modified the total area of the concession.

During the early years of the concession, Aramco not only searched for commercially-producible oil but also delineated overall areas of discovery for future exploitation, to avoid relinquishing land areas with oil and gas potential.

Under the agreement, the concession area extended to adjacent international boundaries whenever applicable. But at that time boundaries with Iraq, Kuwait, the Trucial States (later to become the United Arab Emirates), Oman and Yemen had not been completely settled. Thus Aramco worked only within well-recognized, uncontested boundary lines or borders – the company of course had no authority to involve itself in boundary issues requiring negotiations with other nations.

In the early years, Aramco's exploration budgets were driven by the sharply increasing demand for oil. For economic reasons, exploration and drilling occurred in areas that were considered the best prospects and were closest to our centers of operations.

As world oil demand stabilized, exploration spending would normally be reduced, and as new production was required, of course, we focused our exploration on the most promising areas. Conversely, however, as relinquishment dates approached, we needed to put increased effort into the search for *unprospective* areas (or areas that were *not* promising for the discovery of oil) that could be returned to the Government. Thus these exploration crews were not looking for oil but rather for land areas with *no* oil.[2]

---

of this contract, excepting only that during the life of this contract the Company shall continue to enjoy the right to use the portions so relinquished for transportation and communication facilities, which however shall interfere as little as practicable with any other use to which the relinquished portions may be put."

[2] By 1982, Aramco's concession area amounted to some 220,000 sq. km. [85,000 sq. miles] (189,000 [73,000] onshore and 31,000 [12,000] offshore), with the company having relinquished more than 80 percent of the original area of almost 1.3 million sq. km. [500,000 sq. miles]. See Helen Chapin Metz, ed., *Saudi Arabia: A Country Study*. Washington, D.C.: GPO for the Library of Congress, 1992.

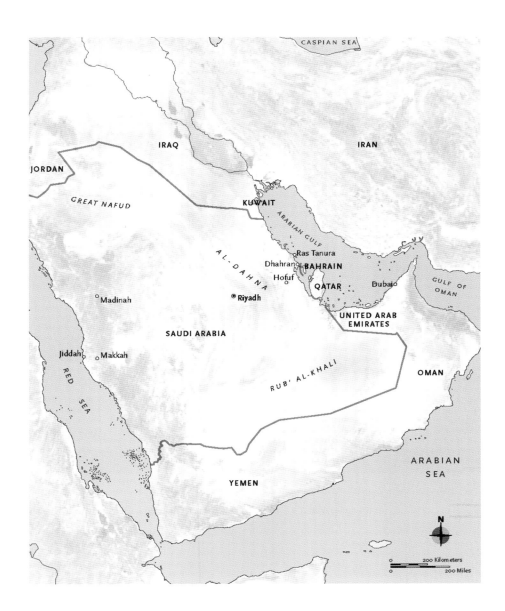

Map of Arabian Peninsula in modern times.

Our teams headed out into areas that were farthest from our operations, which featured the most inhospitable terrain, and which from a geological viewpoint were the least likely to contain productive rocks and formations at any depth.

These exploration efforts employed seismic surveys as well as smaller-diameter structural drills to reach the necessary depths and provide core samples for scientific analysis and proof of unproductivity.

A survey expert at work near Aramco's G-5 exploration camp in Rub' al-Khali in 1969. Photo by B.H. Moody.

We also conducted exploration in areas abutting undetermined borders, so that when the Government eventually negotiated a settlement of these borders, the Kingdom would be able to retain lands in the area that might later prove productive for hydrocarbons.

With these parameters in mind, we moved into a huge unexplored region with unfixed borders known in Arabic as the Rub' al-Khali, or Empty Quarter. This is a vast area of sand about the size of Texas – for the most part impassable and uninhabited desert, with no surface water resources and little animal or plant life, where temperatures could climb as high as 130° F. South and east of this inhospitable area lay the United Arab Emirates, Oman and Yemen, with long stretches of disputed borders. Large parts of Oman, Yemen and the Emirates were under British protection – as "Protectorates" – and the U.K. acted as an advisor to these countries in negotiations to settle their borders with Saudi Arabia. The British had small military forces stationed in these countries – notably in Yemen and Oman – forces that at times patrolled along their version of the borders.

On two occasions in the 1950s, armed British soldiers actually threatened Aramco crews working near the disputed borders. British officers once told our workers: "You have until sundown to get out with all of your equipment." In this case, the British force was based in the southern Yemeni port of Aden, long regarded by Britain as a strategic interest because of the importance of its harbor facilities to British military and commercial vessels.[3] We removed our people as ordered, and the Saudis officially wrote a note of protest to Her Majesty's Government. It took a long time to settle this issue diplomatically. Meanwhile, all the exploration gear that our crews had been unable to remove by the deadline remained abandoned for years in the desert.

It is worth noting that there were a number of other boundary disputes between the U.K. and Saudi Arabia over the years before the international borders between Saudi Arabia and the three countries involved were finally settled.

Aramco's initial exploration effort in the Empty Quarter in the late 1950s identified an area that looked promising for oil discovery called Shaybah. This was a trackless, uninhabited region of towering orange sand dune ranges interspersed with long, gray salt flats or *sabkhas*. Shaybah was about 500 miles (800 kilometers) southeast of Dhahran, which by land in those days would take more than a week to cover because of the inhospitable terrain and the absence of roads. Because of its oil potential, the Shaybah area was excluded from relinquishment, and exploratory drilling was continued at a slow and steady pace, better to delineate the structure.

---

[3] The U.K. finally withdrew from southern Yemen in 1967. The successor to British rule was the pro-Soviet People's Democratic Republic of Yemen (PDRY), often referred to as South Yemen, which eventually merged with North Yemen to form today's Republic of Yemen in 1990.

Shaybah Well No. 1 was drilled in 1968 and struck a very high grade of crude oil in a large reefal structure.

Word of the oil discovery stirred interest in all of the countries that bordered the Saudi Empty Quarter, in the south as well as in the Emirates to the north and east. Geographically, Shaybah was close to Oman, with whom Saudi Arabia had fewer border problems: Only a narrow but difficult mountain range separated Shaybah from the Gulf of Oman.

King Faisal and his Minister of Petroleum, Sheikh Yamani, asked me to meet with the Omanis. The Omani government, the King said, had proposed that the Saudis consider pipelining the Shaybah crude across the Hajar mountain range to a port near Muscat, the closest existing facility. The Omanis offered to provide that

A bulldozer clears the way for the exploration team across the dunes at Shaybah in 1993.

Then and Now

Some 2,500 students, employees of Aramco, in Abqaiq's Opportunity School study English, mathematics, science, blueprint reading, and similar subjects during their working hours and voluntary evening hours. January 1956. Photo by E.E. Seal.

Students gather on the campus of King Abdullah University for Science and Technology, a graduate institution developed by Saudi Aramco, in 2010.

In the picture above from the mid-1950s camels tow an Aramco company car stuck in the soft sand. Below, a camel mother and baby catch a ride in a pickup truck. Photo by Wendy Cocker.

Dammam Well No. 7 blows early traces of oil in 1936. Commercial quantities of crude were discovered in 1938. This photo was taken by pioneer geologist Schuyler B. "Krug" Henry.

Dammam Well No. 7, renamed "Prosperity Well" by Crown Prince (now King) Abdullah, is now a tourist attraction in Dhahran.

A Bedouin on camelback views the Ras Tanura Refinery in the late 1940s.

The Ras Tanura Refinery is seen illuminated at night in 1999. Photo by A.Y. Al-Dobais.

The D.G. Scofield *was the first tanker to load Saudi oil for export in 1939.*

The Leo Star *is a Very Large Crude Carrier (VLCC) in the fleet of Saudi Aramco's shipping arm, Vela International Marine.*

Aramco's Rolling Hills Golf Club course for many years consisted of oiled sand "greens" and desert fairways. Photo by Wendy Cocker.

Saudi Aramco's golf course now uses actual grass irrigated with recycled water.

Aramco pioneer geologist Max Steineke studies a rock for signs that could lead to an oil find, 1935.

Saudi Aramco's earth scientists have the best look yet at the company's productive reservoirs and new prospects in the EXPEC Building's 3-D Visualization Center in Dhahran. Photo by Mark Merzer.

In the 1930s, camels were for the most part beasts of burden. Here some camels in an informal caravan carry bundles of dry grass to market in Riyadh. Photo by Max Steineke.

Today's camels are rarely used to haul loads. More commonly, they are entered in races or "beauty contests." Here some camels avoid the dangers of traffic on busy highways by crossing via a modern overpass. Photo by Wendy Crocker.

Chapter 15
Pricing and Ownership: Part 1

The international pricing system for crude oil and petroleum products, as it existed in the early 1950s, is a complex subject beyond the scope of this book. But by taking a look at the prices of that time and the reasons for them, it should be easier for us to understand why most producing and exporting nations – for example Iran, Venezuela and Mexico – nationalized their original concessionaire companies. Only Saudi Arabia, Kuwait, Bahrain and Abu Dhabi opted for a less confrontational strategy of participation. Saudi Arabia ended up retaining Aramco's trained workforce. Nationalized companies elsewhere lost their management and much of their technology, which had been seconded and supplied by the private owners. When these owners left for home, they took with them most of their employees, whose futures resided with the home enterprise, as well as the expertise they had provided.

As worldwide demand for oil grew during the 1950s, spurred by post-war economic recovery, Aramco and other Middle East producing companies steadily increased production. Major oil companies individually posted prices at $1.80 per barrel for light sweet crude, a level that tended to stabilize as supply and demand coincided worldwide. But toward the end of the decade, supply began exceeding demand, particularly with the Soviet Union stepping up its oil production. Exporting countries were worried about meeting their budgets, and started negotiations with the oil companies to increase prices and/or production.

Before proceeding further, let's further refine our definitions of nationalization and participation as they applied to these negotiations.

- *Nationalization* – This meant the expropriation of all foreign-owned oil operations in the country with little or no compensation. It also resulted in the removal of almost all foreign oil workers, including management and technical employees. The prior owners were required to negotiate prices at which to buy the oil from the country after nationalization. A big disadvantage to the producing country would be the reluctance of buyers to make long-term contractual commitments to buy, when faced with unreliable, bureaucratic government management and weak technological capability. In recent decades, this has been amply demonstrated by declining production due to less-than-optimal operations in countries like Iran, Venezuela, Mexico, Iraq, Russia and many others.

- *Participation* – This term was popularized by the Saudi Minister of Petroleum, Sheikh Yamani, and meant full involvement of the government, financially and managerially, along with the existing shareholders. The extant management system was retained and the new shareholder – the government – was paid with dividends from the profits. In Aramco's case, the primary difficulties of such involvement lay in marketing problems caused by the fact that the four oil-company shareholders were competitors, and of course in how much compensation should be paid to Aramco's owners.

In the early 1950s, Aramco and the Saudi Government reached agreement on a 50–50 profit-sharing arrangement. The Aramco profits were based on the industry-wide price that the four shareholder companies paid Aramco for light sweet crude oil. This was called the posted price. Such an agreement had already been put in place in Venezuela by the individual companies operating there as subsidiaries of their individual American owner companies. The 50-50 profit-sharing arrangement was quickly adopted in other countries. Thus the posted price mechanism became the basis for company-to-government payments worldwide.

During the late 1950s, the oil companies held the posted price at $1.80 per barrel and this remained the basis for the profit split between the companies and the governments. The posted price held, but the actual market price for crude began to fall when growing Soviet production created an oversupply and the actual market price dropped below the posted price. This meant that Aramco was selling crude oil to its shareholders at $1.80 per barrel and paying tax on that basis. Thus the shareholder companies were taking a loss, because they could not sell their newly-purchased crude, nor the products refined from it, for $1.80.

As a result, British Petroleum (BP), successor to the Anglo-Iranian Oil Company, decided to cut its posted price for crude arbitrarily by 10 percent, to $1.62 per barrel. Exxon, one of the Aramco shareholders, followed in early 1960 with a somewhat smaller cut in its global posted price. Aramco, however, was unable to convince the Saudi Government to accept a lower sale price, which would have resulted in reduced tax revenues for the Kingdom. Saudi Arabia and many other producing countries protested these cuts in the posted price as unilateral reductions, lower than had been contemplated in the 50–50 agreements.

Other oil companies were unhappy with BP's and Exxon's actions, and would have preferred prior consultation among the companies – had these types of price discussions not been expressly forbidden by the U.S. Government as violations of American antitrust laws.

As governments stepped up their protests against the unilateral posted price reductions, the major companies began to realize that such price changes required prior review with the countries concerned before they could be implemented.

Subsequent discussions, punctuated by the venting of frustration, led the key producing countries of the developing world to meet in Baghdad about a month after Exxon's posted price cut in 1960 and agree the creation of OPEC.[1] It was clear

---

[1] OPEC was created during a meeting of producer nations September 10–14, 1960, as a

to all that OPEC was formed to enable the producing countries to present a united front in dealing with the oil companies. The lead countries in creating the producers' organization were Saudi Arabia and Venezuela. Abdullah Al-Tariki, the Saudi Minister of Petroleum, who was very vocal and demanding in dealing with Aramco, represented the Saudi Government at the Baghdad meeting.

During the next year as the countries in OPEC became more demanding, Aramco's relationship with Al-Tariki became more difficult. The pressures in OPEC made him more demanding and vocal. Thus numerous issues between the company and the government remained unresolved. In 1962, Crown Prince Faisal assumed increasing operational control of the government, at which point, he named a promising young lawyer, Ahmed Zaki Yamani as Minster of Petroleum. He was a 32 year old native of Mecca who had received part of his legal education in the United States and was no stranger to Aramco. He successfully defended the Company in a law suit filed by a merchant from Hofuf in Shari'a Court.

With Yamani as Minister the government relationship with Aramco became less confrontational and more directed towards settling outstanding issues. Clearly Crown Prince Faisal was taking a more moderate stance vis-à- vis Aramco based upon careful thought and consultation with Yamani. Negotiations with Aramco began , aimed at settling outstanding disputes that had arisen in the Tariki years. The earlier talks had run aground amid confrontational arguments that precluded settlement.

One of the critical issues was a pricing dispute regarding the methods used by Aramco to calculate Tapline profits. Tapline, mentioned earlier, was the company owned by the four Aramco partners that operated a combination 30-inch and 32-inch pipeline from the Arabian Gulf, northwest across the peninsula, through Jordan, Syria and territory occupied by Israel, to the Mediterranean port of Sidon in Lebanon – a total distance of some 1,500 kilometers (930 miles).

---

permanent, intergovernmental organization. Founding members were Iran, Iraq, Kuwait, Saudi Arabia and Venezuela. These were later joined by nine others: Qatar (1961), Indonesia (1962), Libya (1962), United Arab Emirates (1967), Algeria (1969), Nigeria (1971), Ecuador (1973), Gabon (1975) and Angola (2007). From December 1992 to October 2007, Ecuador suspended its membership. Gabon left in 1995. Indonesia suspended its membership in 2009. OPEC currently has 12 members. For its first five years, OPEC had its headquarters in Geneva, Switzerland. The offices were moved to Vienna, Austria in 1965.

Tapline was the first long, fully-constrained pipeline built up to that time (Aramco later built and operated many similar ones). Six pumping stations and associated worker communities were located along the line, and storage and port facilities were installed at Sidon where crude oil was transshipped to the European markets, thereby eliminating the use of the Suez Canal and a long tanker trip around the Arabian Peninsula.

The fully-constrained design was used in lieu of burying the line to prevent expansion and contraction with consequent buckling caused by outside temperature changes. Physically restraining the line from movement greatly lessened expensive burial costs – especially in the Arabian Desert, where daily temperature swings between night and day could vary by 25° C (45° F) or more. Outside daytime temperatures during the summer could reach over 50° C (120° F), and this could be life-threatening.

Bedouins on camels watch a car travel alongside the Tapline pipeline in northern Saudi Arabia. Photo by Bert Seal.

Thus all Tapline (and Aramco) employees were warned about the risks of driving in the desert – especially if they were unfamiliar with desert life. They were told to leave word about their departure point, destination and route traveled. If lost, or when encountering equipment problems, desert travelers were advised to remain with – and preferably under – their vehicles. All company cars and trucks were painted red, so that they could be spotted more easily from the air. Employees were cautioned with utmost seriousness that if they became stranded in the desert, in no case should they wander away from their vehicles.

When I had graduated from my Arabic language program in Lebanon in 1963, after a year and a half of studies, and was set to move back to Saudi Arabia, I decided to send my belongings and part of my family back to Dhahran by air, while I and two young sons drove back to the Kingdom in our own red American station wagon. We followed the gravel washboard road along the Tapline route, traveling from pump station to pump station. It was a very hot afternoon in June. We had driven across the Syrian and Jordanian borders into northern Saudi Arabia and had passed pump station No. 6, at Turaif. We were about halfway to the next station, Badanah, when suddenly we heard a loud clanking noise and the station wagon lurched to a stop. We had lost our crankshaft. Before too long, a large Jordanian truck, bulging with a load of watermelons, appeared on the horizon, heading toward us. When it reached us, the truck stopped, and its Palestinian driver offered to help. After discussing the situation, he reckoned that he would be in Badanah in about 90 minutes, and said he would give the people there a note describing our plight and asking them to send a truck to rescue us and our car. Once we had reached the Badanah pump station, we could be confident that Aramco would send help from Dhahran.

I estimated that help would reach us from Badanah in about four or five hours. The Palestinian driver gave us three or four watermelons to tide us over while we waited. We had also come prepared with plenty of water and food, including a case of small cans of whole-kernel corn, often used by Aramcons on desert excursions as a good source of nutrition and thirst-quenching juice.

During the wait, the boys grew restless – they were tired of lying inside or under the car. So, even though I had earlier cautioned them to stay in the shade, I now suggested that they make a quick run to the pipeline (about 100 yards away) and back again, to give them a little exercise. They were ready to go, and anxious to prove that I had been overly cautious. But the heat was overwhelming, and it was a real physical challenge to run the two hundred yards. When the boys finally returned, panting and on the edge of exhaustion, they were ready to admit how dangerous it was to stray far from one's vehicle when stranded in the desert. The boys then settled down and began to slurp some thirst-quenching watermelon. Eventually a Tapline truck arrived as expected and, as it turned out, we – and the car – lived happily ever after.

Aramco's dispute with the Saudi Government over Tapline focused on the method of determining the taxable profits from moving oil by pipeline to the Mediterranean. After more than a year of negotiations, the dispute was settled in mid-1968, resulting in a large payment to the government and the later conversion of the pipeline company into a subsidiary of Aramco.

As time went on, the countries through which Tapline passed demanded higher and higher fees for crossing their territory. These demands, along with increasing threats of sabotage and concerns over possible Arab–Israeli war in the area, made Tapline a less appealing and thus less profitable option. Maritime shipping technologies had become more attractive, with the design and construction of supertankers too large to pass through the Suez Canal but large enough to be profitable when routed around South Africa's Cape of Good Hope. These huge vessels could transport oil from the Arabian Gulf much more cheaply than the Suez Canal or Tapline options, with all their underlying uncertainties. Aramco moved forward by building and operating its own fleet of supertankers in a company called Vela International Marine, now based in Dubai and a major world tanker operator.

By the mid- to late 1960s, worldwide demand for petroleum products had essentially leveled out. The small amount of growth in demand internationally was soaked up by the beginnings of export production from the Soviet Union. Inflation was rising at a rate of about two and a half to three percent, so OPEC countries were seeing the received value of their $1.80 barrel of crude actually declining.

In 1968, when demand for oil began rising sharply, Yamani formed an organization called OAPEC – the Organization of Arab Petroleum Exporting Countries – to give Arab oil producers more leverage in negotiating pricing with the shareholders of non-Arab OPEC countries. Yamani was well aware of the need to maintain market order. He was also aware of the global political problems that companies and producing nations would face if unilateral price increases by producing nations got out of hand.

At one point, when Libya was pushing up prices into the three-dollar range and threatening oil companies with nationalization, Yamani told me in an airplane conversation that if he could get Aramco to agree to a nine-cent increase in the posted price he could persuade OPEC – not just OAPEC – to hold prices at a level that Aramco shareholders could accept. If, on the other hand, other countries raised their prices first, he felt there might be no way of reining in future increases.

After further discussion with the Minister, I agreed that it would be worth making the effort, and I told him I would do my best to convince the shareholders of the value of letting Yamani move ahead with a nine-cent increase.

Despite my strong recommendation, the shareholders refused. Months of meetings followed. Nerves frayed and tempers flared on both sides as the standoff continued.

At one point, the shareholders questioned whether I was being forceful enough in making their arguments for withholding an increase. They asked that I take one of their representatives with me to see King Faisal and to enunciate once more their position and strong feelings on the matter. They selected George Piercy of Exxon (one of our Aramco directors) to accompany me. He was a very good negotiator and was well known in the industry.

We made the appointment with the King. Of course, Yamani knew Piercy personally and we expected that the Minister would certainly brief the King ahead of the meeting. We went to Riyadh on the day of meeting, and once more I brought along Majed Elass. The three of us sat with the King, had tea and coffee and engaged in minimal conversation. Then, with no preamble, the King said softly: "You know that we need the income." He bluntly asked Piercy, in English: "Tell me, Mr. Piercy, exactly how much oil will your company be buying from Aramco in the next year?"

Startled and obviously unprepared for this question, which was not as a rule discussed with the Government, Piercy stammered in a tight, high-pitched voice: "Your Majesty, predicting oil requirements for our company is very difficult, especially for the future." The King hesitated, nodded, smiled and politely listened to Piercy briefly retelling our story. He then ordered more tea for all. After a few niceties he thanked us for coming – there was no further discussion of the matter that Piercy had intended to discuss with the King at much greater length.

I relate this not as a "putdown" of Piercy, but rather to demonstrate the difficulty – indeed the futility – of trying to challenge an imposing, intelligent monarch like Faisal, a man of few words who was nonetheless well briefed and decisive, and whose mind could not be easily changed once a decision had been made. I have no doubt that Minister Yamani had personally discussed the issues in detail with the King beforehand. Yamani, who did not attend our meeting, was completely trusted by the King, knew the subject matter inside out, and had clearly briefed the monarch well.

The first country to initiate a price increase was Libya, in 1970. By this time, the mercurial Col. Muammar Qaddafi had been in control of the Libyan government for about a year, having deposed the more moderate King Idris in 1969. Libya's rationale for the price hike was that its light crude was more valuable and would command a higher price in Western Europe, which had refineries specially designed for such crude and was thus more capable of absorbing such a price hike. A few months later, Libya imposed output restrictions on its producing companies. In September, Occidental Petroleum agreed to the higher prices, breaking the oil industry's united front, and other companies in Libya followed suit by raising prices to more than $2.50 a barrel. The companies also agreed to higher taxes. The oil majors, realizing that they were being "leapfrogged" by the smaller, weaker companies, felt compelled to acquiesce to price demands in one country after another. (As mentioned earlier, the majors could not discuss these changes with each other ahead of time, because such price talks would have violated U.S. antitrust laws.)

A number of oil companies then entered into discussions with the U.S. Department of Justice and worked out an arrangement allowing them all to meet together to discuss and discourage certain leapfrogging actions, provided that a Justice representative was present to monitor the discussions and make sure that pricing was not mentioned. The leapfrogging involved not only pricing but also other issues not subject to antitrust laws, such as taxation and attempts by some governments to demand various social benefits for local employees.

With the blessing of the Justice Department, the companies met. I attended a number of these meetings in London, which included Aramco's shareholders, BP, Shell and Total. The sessions resulted in a consensus on how the companies could reach agreement on a number of policy issues other than price. These agreements would be negotiated first with countries where the group believed the likelihood of success was greatest. This effort was helpful because it gave some of the smaller companies knowledge about the industry's overall negotiating strategy and encouraged them to reject unreasonable, precedent-setting agreements with countries like Libya, Algeria and other relatively small concessions.

Chapter 16
Pricing and Ownership: Part 2

The London talks were unprecedented in scope and subject matter. Sir Eric Drake, chairman of BP, hosted the discussions at his company's headquarters and often chaired the meetings personally. All the world's major oil companies were represented – in most cases by their CEOs or presidents. There were companies large and small, ranging from the Aramco shareholders to British, French, Italian, Dutch and smaller American companies, as well as other concerns. Even the head of the Gulbenkian family, a powerful force in Middle East petroleum, was represented at the talks.[1] The range of these discussions was remarkable: Each company was having

---

[1] The Gulbenkians made their fortunes by investing in oil ventures in the former Ottoman Empire. Calouste Gulbenkian, a Turkish-born Armenian with British nationality, was instrumental in forming the company that became the Iraq Petroleum Company, and in the merger that created Royal

its own difficulties and had already begun negotiations with the government of the country in which it operated.

In the London meetings, most of the companies had competing interests and each was there to see that its own needs received highest priority. The discussions took place in 1970, prior to the 1971 pricing negotiations in Tehran, Iran. Some of the topics and government demands discussed and defined in London were:

- Participation percentages in different countries
- Equity rights
- Off-take rights by grades of crude
- Differences in taxes by country
- Refining capacity rights and values
- Employee benefits
- Requests by governments for unusual taxes and payments

Typically at these meetings, when I presented the views of my shareholders, I would be asked for details of my negotiations with Minister Yamani and the Saudi Government. The group was very anxious to understand Saudi reactions and counterproposals, if any, because they all believed the Saudi Government was more responsible than, say, Libya's Col. Qaddafi or the Shah of Iran. Outside the Middle East, the risks to the companies were even higher: No one really wanted to initiate discussions in Indonesia, Nigeria, Gabon or Venezuela, where small oil companies could be pressured to make concessions that would set precedence for demands in other countries where large companies would then be forced to make similar concessions.

Iraq, too, was a tough place to work. The Iraq Petroleum Company (IPC) was very strong there and the head of its negotiating team, Jean Duroc-Danner of Compagnie Française des Pétroles or CFP (now known as Total SA), was a very able negotiator who was highly respected and well known in Iraqi government circles. He was able to generate reasonable responses from Iraqi authorities, so he was frequently trusted to begin negotiations in Iraq. Iraqi official responses constituted valuable information, especially to French and British companies.

Duroc-Danner and I would meet frequently to compare notes and reactions, so

---

Dutch Shell. He was also called primary architect of the 1928 Red Line Agreement, which regulated oil company involvement in the post-Ottoman Middle East.

we could improve our understanding of the reasons for the different responses in Iraq and Saudi Arabia. Of course everyone understood the term "participation," but it was hard to determine its relative value in different countries, given differing taxation and accounting methods. So exchanging this kind of information at the London meetings was highly important.

The Iranians, in particular, were the most demanding regarding price increases. Mohammed Reza Pahlevi, the Shah of Iran, who was supported by the U.S. military, was making what were seen then as outlandish demands for prices in the neighborhood of $20 per barrel from the oil company consortium managing the Iranian oil business.[2] The consortium was made up of more than 20 companies, from various countries, which seconded or loaned their employees to the consortium, generally for a two-year term. The short period of work for the consortium meant that the seconded executives and technicians – including the CEO – would do their best to operate the enterprise properly but had very little reason or opportunity to focus on the training and upgrading of Iranian nationals. This resulted in an overstaffed, antagonistic and sullen workforce that also negatively influenced the government and led it to think about ratcheting up oil prices.

The Shah was of course out of step with his people, not only with regard to the oil business but also on a wide range of national economic and social issues. The Iranian people felt that their ruler was not doing enough for them and that he was listening too much to foreigners, who were not only exploiting Iran's natural resources but also, in effect, running that country's military.

The American military was heavily involved in training the Shah's army and supplying it with modern armaments, and was viewed by the Iranian public as having too much influence with – indeed authority over – the Shah's regime. The Americans were perceived as overbearing and insensitive to the needs of the people.

In early 1971, at the Shah's invitation, all 20 or so Iranian consortium member oil companies held a series of meetings in Tehran in an attempt to arrive at a pricing agreement for the country's oil. Since they were part of the same consortium, they could all meet together to arrive at a negotiating position regarding Iranian oil prices without the American participants having to worry about the Sherman Antitrust

---

[2] The consortium was called Iranian Oil Participants Ltd. (IOP). It shared its profits 50-50 with the Iranian government. The Anglo-Iranian Oil Company, which later became British Petroleum (BP), controlled 40 percent of the consortium's shares.

Act. While Aramco itself was not involved in these negotiations, the four Aramco shareholders were members and were invested in the consortium. Minister Yamani, of course, as the Kingdom's OPEC representative, was also involved in the meetings. On two occasions I was invited by our shareholders to travel to Tehran and listen in on some of the discussions – and even take part when legally appropriate.

During one of my visits, the Shah held an audience for the companies, and I was invited to come to the palace with a group of oil company executives led by the Iranian Prime Minister, Dr. Jamshid Amouzegar, who also handled the petroleum portfolio. The visit was only a courtesy call and no negotiations took place. Wearing formal black-tie dress, as instructed, we were ushered into a large audience room, where the Shah was seated at one end on a throne-like chair. He was in full uniform and wore a crown-like head covering. To one side but slightly behind him stood an American general in full dress uniform. While we were there, a steady flow of government officials entered the opulent room, carrying papers and messages to the Shah; when they reached a certain distance from the ruler, they knelt, bowed, delivered their message and then backed away, retreating to the rear of the room, where they exited.

We did not speak with the Shah personally. Instead he made some appropriate remarks of welcome, after which we departed. It seemed to me and to other oil executives there for the first time that the American general and other Westerners were treated with careful deference, compared to the Iranian officials who had to grovel when entering the room.

At any rate, after weeks of negotiation, the meetings with the oil companies in Iran finally produced a signed Tehran agreement in February 1971 that raised the overall crude price in Iran to approximately $2.15 a barrel. The meetings subsequently led to very large price increases in one country after another, with the result that between October 1973 and January 1974 the price went up from $2.15 to as high as $11.65.

Of course, the 1973 oil embargo and worldwide inflation were both accelerating factors, but the eight-dollar jump in the oil price over three to four months was quite a shock for the world economy, which had been used to three decades of prices in a narrow band around two dollars.[3]

---

[3] This was the oil embargo implemented by the Organization of Arab Petroleum Exporting Countries (OAPEC), including Saudi Arabia, in response to the U.S. military intervention on the side of Israel in the October War of 1973. The embargo will be explored in detail in the next chapter.

By 1972, Saudi Oil Minister Yamani had finally convinced some members of OPEC to push for a united front on participation. The major foreign oil companies operating in the Gulf, seeing no alternative, agreed to open serious participation discussions with the region's governments during the spring and summer of 1972. During that period, we of course were engaged in negotiations with the Government of Saudi Arabia. These negotiations were so unprecedented that tempers flared at times among the four shareholder companies, who were trying to salvage the best they could from their Aramco ownership.

At one point in 1971, I, as the negotiator, was asked to carry the shareholder message to the Government. Once again, there was some concern that perhaps I had not previously conveyed this message forcefully enough or clearly enough, so the shareholders decided to send a letter to King Faisal explaining their desires and their needs. They asked the then-president of Aramco, Liston Hills (whom I succeeded a few months later), to present the letter to the King and to assist me with the discussions as needed.

Liston and I flew to Riyadh on a very hot, windy and dusty day. The sand was flying and visibility was poor. A car from our Riyadh office delivered us to the meeting with the King. We sent the car back to the office, thinking that the conversation could last some time, and told the driver we would phone him when we were ready to leave. We met with King Faisal and Yamani. Hills sat next to the King and I beside Hills. Yamani sat on the other side of the room, for the most part silent and listening. Liston told the King that we had been asked to deliver a letter from the shareholders and that we would be grateful if he would consider it. The King took the sealed envelope and set it on a table beside his chair while we talked pleasantries. It was really a very nice, friendly discussion of a number of unrelated topics. There was no further mention of the letter that obviously contained the well-known shareholder positions on participation.

Finally the King said he had to leave, and the subject of the letter did not come up again. As the King stood, we too rose to our feet, as did Minister Yamani, and we all left the room. Yamani offered to drive us to the airport in his car, rather than have us call ours. He suggested that Liston sit in the back and that I sit up front with him. As he drove down the road, he reached into his robe and pulled out the envelope we had given to the King – it had been opened! – and he said with a smile, "Perhaps you could use this." We drove on to the airport.

So much for delivering a letter to the King! Neither Liston nor I had seen Yamani take the letter from the King, and we were quite surprised that he had it in hand as we left the room. Apparently Yamani had opened and read the letter as we walked to the car. He was aware that both Hills and I knew the King himself would not open the letter. The Saudis knew I would understand from this that King Faisal had entrusted Yamani to be his negotiator on this matter and that he, the King, had no need to read any further restated arguments. The affair had been handled in this indirect manner because the King did not want to embarrass us by being openly negative.

The participation negotiations of the oil companies and producing countries continued during the spring and summer of 1972, with the largest and longest session occurring at Beit Meri, a summer resort in the mountains of Lebanon. By October 1972, the negotiations had reached agreement based on a draft proposed by the Aramco legal staff, which granted 25 percent participation to the producing countries. The oil companies agreed to the pact and on December 20, 1972, Saudi Arabia and Abu Dhabi signed the agreement, effective January 1, 1973. Kuwait and Qatar signed in the following month.

Ownership participation was to increase incrementally to 51 percent by 1982, in what both sides anticipated would be a relatively stable process of maintaining prices and managing ownership. What actually happened was quite different: The Libyans again broke ranks and extracted 60 percent participation rather quickly from their smaller companies, and in time the Saudis and the others followed.

From the very beginning, the Aramco–Saudi Government participation agreement (and subsequent modifications) contained provisions under which Aramco could call upon its prior shareholders for technical assistance, for which appropriate compensation would be paid.

Various different types of agreement were signed in other countries. Some, like Abu Dhabi and Kuwait, were quite similar to the Aramco accord, but in most other prominent cases – such as Iran, Libya, Iraq, Venezuela, Colombia, Mexico and Algeria – the companies were actually nationalized.

Aramco had helped develop the most effective and smoothest transition to national ownership that the world oil industry had seen. Rather than acrimoniously severing ties with the Western companies that had developed its oil industry, as had happened in other producing countries, Saudi leaders made sure the successor company – Saudi Aramco – maintained important commercial and technical relationships with the former American shareholders. This harmonious process not only demonstrated the trust and close coordination between company and government as both grew to relative maturity, but also created an atmosphere conducive to future joint ventures and cooperation between Saudi Arabia and the global energy industry – a valuable advantage for the Kingdom in its march toward national development.

Chapter 17
The Oil Embargo

The fourth Arab–Israeli War began on October 6, 1973, with the Egyptian and Syrian armies launching simultaneous attacks on Israel. The Israelis called it the Yom Kippur War because it began on that Jewish holy day. The Arabs called it the Ramadan War, because it was fought during the holy month of fasting. With menacing Israeli armor beginning to move toward their borders, Egypt and Syria had decided to carry out a preemptive surprise strike. Israel found its defenses breeched, especially in the Sinai, where the Egyptian forces successfully crossed the Suez Canal and quickly began advancing eastward across the Sinai Peninsula toward the Israeli border. The Arab world, stung with a humiliating military defeat in the 1967 War (in which Israel had launched the first strike), was suddenly jubilant, and the masses, even in Saudi Arabia, were out in the streets cheering.

But for the Arabs, the thrill of potential victory was short-lived. Israel was clearly in crisis, and it called for help from its closest ally, the United States. So serious were Israel's losses in the Sinai that President Nixon authorized the Pentagon to begin a major airlift of military hardware to the Israelis. Nixon also placed U.S. forces on a worldwide alert.[1] The Soviet Union placed seven airborne divisions on alert. Secretary of State Henry Kissinger and others were reportedly worried that if Israel were on the brink of defeat, it would use its "secret" arsenal of tactical nuclear weapons against the Arabs, possibly precipitating World War III.

The U.S. initiated a resupply effort for Israel called Operation Nickel Grass. Hundreds of flights of American C-141 Starlifter and C-5 Galaxy aircraft soon began landing in Israel with tons of weaponry and equipment. The tide of battle turned and Arab excitement rapidly changed to dismay. New levels of bitterness and anger were directed toward America.

Aramco's discussions with Petroleum Minister Ahmed Zaki Yamani on participation became more difficult, as a number of OPEC countries began threatening outright nationalization and proceeded with ownership plans. The producing nations focused on taking over oil concessions run mostly by American and European oil companies. Some producing countries even began raising oil prices unilaterally, without OPEC's agreement.

King Faisal was shocked to see the United States taking a blatantly pro-Israeli stance in the U.N. Security Council, vetoing all condemnations of aggressive Israeli actions and of Israel's ongoing occupation of Arab lands in the guise of defense. At times even the Russians were siding with Israel's position.

I had been involved in a number of discussions with King Faisal in the months leading up to the October War, and was surprised to hear him suggest – and more and more begin to believe – that there must be a Zionist–Communist conspiracy that was compelling the United States to condone this injustice and the unjustified seizure of Palestinian land. What else, he would argue, could cause such blind acceptance of Israel's misdeeds? He came to this conclusion because many of the key founders of socialism and communism in Europe and particularly Russia were

---

[1] *White House Memorandum of Conversation: Israeli Ambassador to the U.S. Simcha Dinitz et al. and U.S. Secretary of State Henry Kissinger et al.,* October 9, 1973. Transcript, George Washington University National Security Archive.

of Jewish ancestry, including Marx, Trotsky and Lenin.

At one point the King began to question me, asking why American business was not doing more to influence public opinion in the U.S. and why we were not prodding our government to change its policy toward Israel, which continued to ignore U.N. resolutions with impunity. Israel, he noted, was pressing ahead with its program of expanding control and de facto ownership of the most desirable lands in the Occupied Territories by building new Israeli settlements.

Finally, in one of our meetings, King Faisal stated simply and bluntly that I, as head of Aramco, had failed to persuade our shareholder companies to present this case more forcefully to the American media and public.

I reminded him of several instances in which we had approached the press and sought to win exposure for the Arab viewpoint. But he remained adamant, expressing his words quietly but firmly. While he spoke on this subject, the King kept plucking at his camelhair robe, as he would do whenever agitated or upset.

King Faisal remained unconvinced that American industry – already losing business from those Arab countries that were now boycotting imports of American products – was doing enough to tell the story and influence public opinion. The American government's pro-Israel policy was uniting all Arabs against the United States. The Arab people felt great sympathy for the grievances of the Palestinians – specifically, Israel's illegal annexation of Arab land, the lack of recognition of rights of the Palestinian people, and America's vetoing of U.N. efforts to deal with boundaries and other Arab–Israel issues. As he pressed his case, the King became quite loquacious and forceful on the subject – not his usual manner.

Majed Elass, as an Arabic-speaking executive on our Board, had once again accompanied me to my meeting with the King. As we left the audience, after hearing King Faisal's impassioned appeal, both of us knew that we needed to undertake a major initiative immediately – something that would convince the King that Aramco and its shareholders were doing all they could to present the Arab position and feelings to the American business community and public.

In May 1973, about six months before the Arab–Israeli War broke out, I decided to make a trip across the United States, visiting the CEOs of as many of the largest American corporations as I could, to tell them this story, to present the Arabs' feelings and resentment over U.S. policy and to explain the grave potential consequences of a boycott as well as the even more disastrous possibility of nationalization.

My goal was to impress upon these corporate leaders the importance of the King's message, to ensure that U.S. business maintained its position in a large and growing regional market. In all, I met with 38 chief executives. We visited them in New York, Detroit, Milwaukee, San Francisco, Los Angeles, Dallas and Houston. Sometimes we would meet with the CEOs of more than one company together in one room. For example, I brought Henry Ford II of the Ford Motor Company and Tom Murphy, chairman of General Motors, together for breakfast. We picked the biggest banks and largest industries, including IBM, General Electric, Bank of America, First National City Corp, Allis-Chalmers and a large group of executives in Milwaukee. I also met with the oil companies.

The oil company chairmen I met with, especially those from the Aramco shareholder companies, were the most active in spreading the word about the Arab position. In return, they received a tremendous amount of criticism and negative publicity in the United States. In fact, there was a riot outside Socal headquarters in San Francisco, with protesters throwing garbage and eggs at the building. All this received a great deal of unfavorable U.S. press coverage – the pro-Israel lobbying machinery had been very active indeed.

The essence of my argument in my discussions with the chief executives was that oil was important to the United States, and that American business interests around the world were being harmed by our country's negative image in the Middle East and elsewhere. Our Arab–Israel policy was anything but evenhanded, and it favored an Israeli government that refused to engage peacefully with its neighboring Arab states. I reminded some CEOs that their companies' own products were already being boycotted in the Middle East because of American policies and because their company actions were seen as favoring Israel. Subject to the Arab League's boycott at the time were Coca-Cola, Ford and other well-known brands.

We eventually returned to Saudi Arabia, and I went to see the King to brief him in considerable detail on what I had done. He listened patiently, and then asked, "How did the companies react?" I said that generally they had reacted very well. I proceeded to tell him about many of them, especially the Aramco shareholder companies, which had undertaken very positive public relations measures, including placing ads in newspapers and magazines emphasizing the need for evenhandedness and peace in the Middle East.

The King was very probing about which companies were not being cooperative.

I tried to avoid answering these questions, but he went down the list of companies to find out which were the most cooperative and which the least. He scanned the list, settled on one and asked: "I see you met with Mr. Ford. Was he cooperative?" I replied that Ford had come to the meeting. The King smiled. Of course Ford Motor Company was already subject to industrial boycott by many Arab countries because it had overtly assisted Israel.[2] Henry Ford II certainly was not in tune with the Arab side of the problem. He seemed surprised that not a single Ford automobile could be seen in Saudi Arabia, Syria or Jordan in those days, simply because they had opened a facility in Israel. He asked me in later correspondence if I could advise him how Ford could get off the boycott list. I replied that there was nothing I or Aramco could do about this and that essentially it was his problem.

Incidentally, Coca-Cola was also subjected to the boycott in the Arab world because it had opened facilities in Israel. A bit later, the existing Coca-Cola bottling company in Saudi Arabia, owned by the Kaki family, received approval from Coca-Cola to change the name of its product to Kaki-Kola. They then began bottling and selling the product under this new name. The same Arabic letter, *ka*, is used for both the hard *c* and *k* of English, so, visually, the Arabic logo for Kaki-Kola was not much of a change from *Coca-Cola*.

The King acknowledged our effort with the major banks, but he knew as well as I did that our impact on them would be minimal. At the end of the discussion, he thanked me, and I felt sure that he understood we had made a determined effort.

Despite our efforts and some very positive responses from industry, America's pro-Israel policy did not change. King Faisal began to think more and more about initiating an oil embargo. He was looking for a way to remind the U.S. Government and the world that the Palestinian Arabs had not caused, nor were they involved in, the Holocaust of World War II, the murderous Nazi campaign of persecution against the Jews. So why had the Palestinians been made to pay the price for a tragedy not of their making, by being

---

[2] Later, in 1977, Israel's supporters in Congress secured passage of several "anti-boycott laws" as amendments to the Export Administration Act and the 1976 Tax Reform Act, which made it illegal for U.S. firms to cooperate with the Arab boycott of Israel. Companies could face fines for even acknowledging the existence of the Arab boycott, leading some companies to ask, "What boycott?"

uprooted from their homes and from land they had owned for many generations? And why was the U.S. supplying Israel with arms and money so the Israelis could conquer and acquire more land, without giving a single thought to fairness or honesty or concern for the displaced Palestinians? Whenever the issue of Israeli misbehavior was raised in the U.N. Security Council, the United States exercised its veto power against resolutions critical of Israel, and in most cases was the only nation to do so. King Faisal had no basic hatred of the Jews – he was frustrated and angered by what he saw as a blind American policy that allowed Israel to run amok in the Middle East.

Surprisingly, the King did not mention any discussions with the State Department or with Secretary of State Kissinger on the Palestinian problem or on the oil embargo threat. We knew, however, that U.S. Ambassador James E. Akins had had a number of such discussions and seemed to be personally empathetic with King Faisal's views. Akins' later writings reflect this. He had warned more than a year beforehand that Saudi Arabia and other nations were poised to restrict oil shipments. Akins was later fired by Secretary Kissinger, reportedly because of his excessive partiality to Saudi Arabia.[3]

I had a number of discussions with Yamani and the King regarding their consideration of an oil embargo. During each of these conversations, I voiced my doubts that an embargo could be implemented worldwide in such a way as to restrict the importation of oil to certain targeted countries only. In my view, an oil embargo was not likely to be as effective as they hoped. Nonetheless, King Faisal continued to bring the subject up, either through Yamani or directly with me.

Finally, during my last discussion with the King about a possible embargo, I said I just could not understand how he would be able to implement such a plan successfully. The King looked at me and replied: "I am not going to do it. You are. Aramco will do it."

On Thursday, October 18, 1973, a few days after this discussion with King Faisal, a weekend broadcast over official Radio Riyadh carried an announcement of King Faisal's decision to reduce oil production, effective immediately and lasting until the end of November. The initial reduction would be 10 percent.

------

[3] Douglas Martin, "James E. Akins, Envoy to Saudi Arabia, Dies at 83," *The New York Times*, July 24, 2010.

After this official broadcast, there was no need for us to wait for further details or instructions. Aramco immediately began to shut down production sufficiently to implement the decision. The important thing for our company was to be viewed as complying with the Government and not ignoring a Royal Decree. The day after King Faisal's order, President Nixon asked Congress to supply Israel with $2.2 billion-worth of military assistance. The King's response was "to halt oil exports to the U.S. for taking this position." At that point, the last oil tanker bound for America had just finished loading and was underway. A second tanker destined for the U.S. was loading at the port, but was rerouted to Rotterdam.

Three days later, Aramco received its first formal instructions on the embargo from the Government: We were invited to Riyadh to meet with Minister Yamani. I took with me our comptroller Fred M. Moffett, as well as a company lawyer and an operations executive. We traveled to the capital and entered the Petroleum Minister's office. Yamani had three or four able people there, all of whom we knew. The Minister announced that the total embargo against the U.S. would be in addition to the general reduction of 10 percent. This brought the total reduction in our oil exports to 25 percent. Yamani said the Government would divide all other countries into categories. The first category would be the most-favored nations, including the Arab states, the U.K., Spain, France and those African states that had broken off relations with Israel. States in the first category were permitted to buy oil in the usual quantities, with the understanding that it was not to be transshipped elsewhere. All other countries would be embargoed or would receive their pro-rata share of the remaining production based upon their demonstrated political cooperation as evaluated by the Saudi Government.

The Netherlands, for example, joined the United States on the *fully embargoed* list. But the Dutch port of Rotterdam – the only port in Europe that could handle the very largest tankers – could be used to transship oil to other designated, "unembargoed" countries after offloading. Aramco was assigned the task of ensuring that oil offloaded worldwide was not transshipped to non-designated recipients. We were required to certify that each barrel went to its intended destination. This required that we set up a small and very capable group that included our chief financial officer, Fred Moffett, as well as Hal Fogelquist, then vice president of Corporate Planning and Administration, and Joe Johnston, the head of Aramco's New York office. This group would designate, document and verify that every shipment ended up at its stipulated destination. The New York office would work with the shareholder companies in an effort to resolve the problems they faced distributing oil they had bought for resale.

Yamani's office had also created its own small group headed by a Ministry of Petroleum employee (and one of his key aides), Khader Herzallah, a talented and trusted Saudi national of Palestinian origin who received instructions directly from the Petroleum Minister's office, which in turn reported directly to the King. Changes were permitted frequently, whenever embargoed countries reached satisfactory political agreements with Saudi Arabia.

The Aramco group would then make the required adjustments in deliveries of oil worldwide, and report the results upon completion. The loading and offloading of tankers and their rerouting, along with accommodating shifting crude grades, etc., became a major and highly-confidential scheduling problem. The Aramco shareholder companies, who were the primary buyers and shippers, needed to adjust the make-up of their cargoes to conform to changing allocations and destinations. The overall result was a constant shifting and rerouting of tankers and offloading, all carefully documented, to the final agreed location. Aramco operations in turn dealt with the oil tankers waiting to be loaded. These tankers were subject to adjustments in what they took on – the correct mix of products had to be determined amid ever-changing designations.

In the end, I had to admit to myself that the King had given me the right response when I had insisted this couldn't be done. He knew that Aramco could do it. Aramco had the track record.

As the oil embargo continued, the United States was winding down its war in Vietnam, and word reached us shortly after the enactment of the embargo that the U.S. Navy was running short of jet fuel for its naval aircraft at a time when the fleet was engaged in a rapidly-changing war effort.

Exxon Chairman John Kenneth "Ken" Jamieson had been contacted by the U.S. Defense Department and asked whether he thought Aramco might approach King Faisal and ask for a "dispensation" from the oil embargo for the U.S. Navy in the war zone. Jamieson passed this request on through Joe Johnston at Aramco New York, who said the thinking was that perhaps I could discuss this matter personally with the King. As a result, I was asked to make a trip back to the U.S. to meet with Pentagon officials to determine what they needed and where. With this background, I would be able to present the Navy's dilemma to the King.

I met briefly with Defense Secretary James R. Schlesinger and Deputy Secretary

William P. "Bill" Clements, whom I knew well from his time as head of a large oil drilling company, SEDCO. Clements and I then went to his office to work on the problem. The Pentagon wondered if there was any way I could prevail upon the Saudis to supply jet fuel to the U.S. Navy in the Vietnam area in such a way that would secretly avoid the boycott. A high-level official U.S. request to Saudi Arabia would be politically awkward, they said. It would be better if I could approach the Saudis informally, arguing on the basis of a critical Navy need. We worked out their jet fuel needs and where the product transfer could take place. I told Clements that I would talk to the King and Minister Yamani about this. I felt that, even if I received a go-ahead, Aramco would be required to break its own embargo secretly and in such a way that some of our own people would not know an exception was being made.

After my meetings in Washington, D.C., I returned to Saudi Arabia and went to see King Faisal and Yamani. I explained the situation to them, which was, of course, that the U.S. was at war in Vietnam and needed jet fuel mainly to allow the Navy to refuel its aircraft on aircraft carriers off the coast of Southeast Asia. I said that I had been briefed on the Navy's fuel requirements in detail, and felt it was probably in all of our interests that King Faisal and Aramco make this one exception to the embargo. I said that I realized that the exception had to be made secretly, and that we were prepared to work this out in such a way that there would be no publicity.

I assured the King that we understood his thinking – that the real goal of the oil embargo was to produce a shift in the pro-Israel policy of the United States. I also pointed out that even if the embargo were successful, changes in U.S. policy would not occur in time to resolve the immediate supply problem for the American war effort in Vietnam.

The King listened carefully. "Are you telling me that this approach to me is not being instigated by the oil companies?" I affirmed it was not, and said the request came directly from the U.S. Government.

"Well, I don't understand how you are going to do this," King Faisal said. "God help you." Translation: We should proceed, but under no circumstances should we get caught and have this erupt as a public issue. The secret of the U.S. Navy's "exception" was effectively kept under wraps for a number of years afterward. Secretary of State Kissinger and the U.S. Ambassador to Saudi Arabia were not involved in the direct discussions, though presumably they were later informed of the plan by the Defense Department when the time was right.

We needed to develop a scheme to allow us to break our own embargo without our own people knowing there was an exception. Aramco's procedures were so tight that our people were under specific instructions for the handling of every tanker, including its departure and arrival at its destination. We knew at all times exactly what oil was going where, and there were to be no exceptions. Our problem now was to make an exception without anyone involved knowing about it!

We decided to load a Caltex tanker out of the Bahrain harbor (not out of our own terminal) with jet fuel, and then secretly offload the cargo onto another Caltex ship. These were medium-range (MR) tankers, carrying between 240,000 and 400,000 barrels of product. To complicate the clandestine operation, the second ship was not to be aware of its destination until after it was underway.

The transfer was made as planned. Later we were informed that rumors were circulating about an exception being made to the embargo. We checked with officials at Socal, a Caltex owner, and they were adamant they had not leaked anything. We finally determined that the information leaks occurred somewhere within the Caltex organization. The Saudi Government was informed of the leak, but fortunately the press never picked up the information, and embargo-busting jet fuel was safely delivered to the U.S. Navy.

As the oil embargo continued, oil prices began to rise sharply, because the market anticipated shortages in the many countries subject to the embargo – who were trying to buy elsewhere, knowing that Aramco had cut production. The embargoed countries immediately began to negotiate with Saudi Arabia, seeking removal from the list by such means as offering to apply pressure on Israeli policies regarding Palestine, facilitating Saudi access to various commercial markets and providing diplomatic support for the Kingdom in United Nations dealings.

In countries that managed to get relief from the embargo, worried customers immediately began to build inventory, ordering more crude and products to guard against future scarcities. As a result, demand for Aramco production began to increase to a maximum level of 9.5 to 10 million barrels per day. Prices climbed from about $5 a barrel to as high as $27 a barrel. To simplify the arithmetic, this meant about $300 million per day in 1974 dollars had to be paid to Aramco by its four shareholders, who were also our primary customers, and this was causing them liquidity problems. Aramco in turn had to pay the Saudi Government both royalties and taxes of roughly 50 percent, in addition to its own expenses and new capital costs, and then to promptly remit the remaining balance to the four shareholders as dividends. Of course, the Government's primary revenue source was the Aramco remittance, which was accompanied by a reporting of the Aramco taxes and royalties.

Since all parties involved were faced with fast-changing liquidity problems, we held monthly EXCOM meetings to declare dividends, followed by conference calls with the Ministry of Finance and major world banks so that the funds could be transferred to the correct accounts. To oversimplify, the movements of these funds were for the most part done simultaneously to minimize cash movements between banks, some of which serviced more than one party.

While the logistics of moving these large sums of money was a tremendous problem, the banks became concerned over how to invest this cash. The Saudi Government and those of other producing countries needed some of these funds to finance domestic projects, but these projects were controlled by various government departments whose timing requirements varied greatly. Thus the cash accumulated in banks. Government planning and spending were constantly changing because the governments too were dependent upon oil markets, and oil prices were being buffeted by constant company-to-government negotiations.

In the case of a large producer like Aramco, the banks made worried efforts to keep abreast of the latest timing requirements. I recall a visit to the Kingdom by David Rockefeller and his retinue from Chase Manhattan Bank, who spent an evening at my house in Dhahran. They just wanted to discuss the world as we saw it. Their big concern was where to lend the large quantities of accumulated funds that they held on behalf of the Kingdom, with the dollar being hit by rising inflation and with growing uncertainties about the timing of loans. The big banks were looking for places to lend, and they turned to developing countries like Brazil that were building huge dams and electrification projects – with payouts in the future from governments with varying degrees of stability.

We did our best to give banks as much information as possible as a matter of self-interest, but we knew that the world banking community was in for a rough ride, which was certainly borne out later.

During the months following the 1973 Arab–Israeli War and the ongoing oil price increases, the American news media were very active in covering the Middle East and its energy industry. Most major news outlets, of course, were very much pro-Israel and anti-oil company. They echoed the public's understandable anger over the unprecedented price hikes at the gasoline pumps.

During this period, Aramco's New York office was deluged with media phone calls requesting interviews with Aramco officials when they were in the United States or asking to visit company headquarters in Saudi Arabia. Although Aramco was slow to accept such requests, when visits and interviews were granted we made our best efforts to show the company and the country of Saudi Arabia in a fair and accurate light. High-level U.S. congressmen and senators were also visiting Saudi Arabia during this period and, while there, often requested meetings with Aramco management and tours of our oil facilities. Among the senators interested in visiting Aramco were such prominent figures as Sen. Jacob Javits of New York and Sen. Edward Kennedy of Massachusetts.

Frank Jungers welcomes visiting Massachusetts Senator Edward (Ted) Kennedy to Dhahran.

One important media request for a visit and interview came from Mike Wallace of CBS News' popular *60 Minutes* – a magazine-style public affairs program known for its tough, investigative approach and hard-hitting interviews. Mike Wallace was well known as a frequent, sometimes harsh, critic of Arab governments and their policies. But we felt this important television news venue would give Aramco an opportunity to present its case to the American public, so we agreed to the request. When Wallace arrived in Dhahran, we put him up in one of our guest houses and arranged for him to tour the company's facilities, including some typical oil installations. I also scheduled a breakfast and a morning interview with him.

Wallace and his crew set up to film and record the interview for *60 Minutes*. He asked questions about the oil embargo and why Aramco, then owned by American oil companies, could not prevent the embargo by taking a firmer and more "patriotic" stance. I responded by explaining that I had argued clearly and distinctly against

CBS Newsman Mike Wallace interviews Frank Jungers for 60 Minutes.

the embargo in my discussions with the Saudi leadership, but when the Ruler of Saudi Arabia made his decision, any refusal by Aramco to implement the embargo would endanger oil supplies worldwide and jeopardize America's access to them. In answering Wallace's questions, I sought to correct erroneous impressions about our company and the Kingdom – of which there were many. I suggested that after our discussion, when he toured our facilities, he should feel free to talk to and openly ask reasonable questions of any employee he encountered, whether American or Arab. My staff observers at the interview also recorded our discussions, which lasted over two hours. The interview was conducted in a positive atmosphere with occasional humor. As we concluded, Wallace agreed that he would consider sending me a copy of the taped interview.

After the interview was over and the camera had stopped rolling, Wallace remarked that he had been unaware that the company's workforce contained such a large percentage of Saudi employees. He said he had gotten the impression from my remarks that we were replacing Americans with Saudis in many key technical and administrative jobs. He wondered whether this policy was wise.

I told him we believed it was important to utilize and train local labor whenever possible. To bring this point home more effectively, I suggested that we modify his itinerary somewhat and send him by car to our southern community at Abqaiq, about one and a half hours away. (Abqaiq was the center of operations for our largest onshore oilfields.) There he would meet the manager of our southern operations, Ali Al-Naimi, who would show him the facilities and host him to dinner. In this way, Mike Wallace could make his own assessment of our operations and of Saudi capabilities. He agreed, so we quickly notified Ali Al-Naimi of the change in plans, which he of course was willing to accommodate.

The trip to Abqaiq and other elements of Wallace's visit went off well. Later, after his return to Dhahran, the CBS newsman thanked me, saying that he appreciated our hospitality. He was impressed with what he had seen of Aramco and its people, especially Ali Al-Naimi and his workforce.

I later learned that Ali and his wife, Dhabyah Ahmed Al-Naimi, had hosted a small dinner for Mike Wallace at their home, during which an inevitable discussion ensued on the Middle East and its problems. Apparently, the hostess, Dhabyah – who was completely fluent in English – reacted sharply to some comments by Wallace that she felt were anti-Arab. She challenged the CBS newsman, asking why he – and indeed almost all members of the major American media – took biased positions against the Arabs, especially on the Palestinian question, which involved a clear denial of a people's rights. She also asked why the U.S. press was silent about Israel's expropriation of Palestinian lands. Wallace was apparently quite taken aback by this unexpected challenge. Nevertheless, the dinner conversation returned to normal, and the evening ended most cordially. When I saw him before he left, Wallace did not comment specifically on Mrs. Al-Naimi's dinner-table broadside, saying merely that he was most impressed by the Al-Naimis and had enjoyed their company that evening in Abqaiq.

Months went by as we waited patiently for the Mike Wallace interview to appear on *60 Minutes*. In those days before global satellite television, the program had to be taped in New York and flown to Dhahran for our later viewing. When it was finally broadcast in the United States, the Aramco segment merited less than two minutes and was completely innocuous in content. Mike Wallace had found nothing negative or sensational to report about Aramco and he was certainly not about to repeat Mrs. Al-Naimi's stinging dinner comments about the American news media and the Palestinians.

Chapter 18
Faisal's Vatican Overture

During the 1960s, the Catholic Near East Welfare Association (CNEWA), an agency of the Vatican, was very active in the Arab countries of the Middle East. One of its core mandates was to provide humanitarian assistance to those in need, without regard to nationality or creed. The organization, established in 1926 by Pope Pius XI, was now responding to the numerous problems facing displaced Palestinians, many of whom had been expelled from their homes during wars with Israel and more of whom were continuing to lose their lands to Israeli expropriation in the occupied West Bank and Gaza Strip.

Palestinian refugees received basic assistance from the U.N. Relief and Works Agency (UNRWA), which provided refugee camps for those driven from their homes. But UNRWA funding was inadequate, and sometimes the U.N. could not provide even the minimum assistance necessary to feed and house the alarming, ever-swelling number of refugees. Children desperately needed more and better schooling, both inside and outside the Occupied Territories. Palestinian bitterness and anger were spreading to all the Arab and Muslim states.

The head of CNEWA, Monsignor (later Bishop) John G. Nolan, traveled throughout the Middle East raising funds for the refugees. I first met him in Lebanon, while I was studying Arabic at Shemlan. Nolan was a dynamic and creative Catholic priest who was obviously a rising star and well thought of in church leadership circles. Over a number of years he made many trips to Aramco in Saudi Arabia, where he became well known and was admired by Americans and Saudis alike. Later, when the Pope established Bethlehem University in the West Bank specifically to provide higher education for Palestinians, Nolan and CNEWA furnished assistance to the De La Salle Christian Brothers, a teaching order of Catholic clerics responsible for running the university and educating its students in the face of serious Israeli interference.

In early 1972, amid growing world tensions that would lead to the Arab–Israeli War the following year, Msgr. Nolan made a trip to Dhahran to meet with me and discuss an idea that he was convinced could help the Palestinians and perhaps make Israel pay closer attention to world opinion.

Nolan believed that if Saudi Arabia and the Vatican could establish formal diplomatic relations with each other, this would be viewed throughout the Arab world as a great policy triumph for the Kingdom. A strengthening of relations between Catholics and Muslims could unnerve the Israeli government and cause it to rethink its hostile stance toward the Palestinians.

The monsignor was confident he could present his idea to the highest levels in the Vatican. He wondered if I would raise the question with King Faisal. His suggestion was that the two countries exchange initial visits by prominent representatives, to become better acquainted and discuss the possibility of formal diplomatic relations.

After considerable thought I agreed, and made an appointment with King Faisal to present the idea to him. He appeared to like the possible positive effects of this proposal. The King had heard of Nolan and his good work, and he questioned me about Nolan's reliability, discretion and influence.

I vouched for Nolan, for his work and for our friendship. But I said that he had not given me any indication as to which Catholic prelate, if any, in the Vatican he might have approached, and whether indeed church officials would like the idea. I said I

heads of state, such as the President of Lebanon and the King of Jordan. But obviously this tragedy had occurred unexpectedly and, due to the limited time frame, a number of leaders from distant lands had been forced to send high-level substitutes.

We were unaware of the specifics of the day's program, so we waited, and spent our time people-watching, studying the distinguished incoming arrivals. Idi Amin, the President of Uganda, arrived in fully formal military attire, armed with a pistol and holster. He was accompanied by a young son, about 10 years old or even less, who wore an exact copy of his father's uniform except that his holstered pistol was a toy one. Amin and his son walked past us to their seats and we exchanged pleasantries.

The seating area filled rather slowly, doubtless due to delays at the airport. Meanwhile we all wondered what kind of ceremony awaited us. We were sitting quietly when all of a sudden two military officers approached Majed and me, asking us to follow them quickly and to "keep ahead of everybody." We followed them to the center of the open square. As we got there, the gates opened and a group of men entered, some of them carrying a bier on which lay the covered body of the King. The bearers were sons of the King. We were motioned to move forward quickly, which we did, and I expressed my condolences to each of the sons, particularly to Prince Saud Al Faisal, Deputy Minister at the Ministry of Petroleum, whom I knew best, (later in 1975, he became Minister of Foreign Affairs, a position he still holds), and Prince Turki Al Faisal, who later became head of Saudi Intelligence. The two men were very openly grieving, and tears rolled down their faces. They thanked me warmly.

As the procession moved to the center, Ahmed Abdul Wahhab intercepted me. He informed me that, after the ceremony, the Muslim guests would accompany the family to the mosque for prayers. After the prayers, only members of the family would proceed to the burial ground. He suggested we move quickly to a waiting car that would take us to the airport, where our plane was first in line and ready for departure. I thanked Ahmed for his thoughtfulness and help in these most difficult times, and we then hurried to the car. On the trip back to Dhahran, Majed and I talked, reviewing these profoundly moving two days. We discussed the unusual delay in the burial of the King to the day following his death. Neither of us had seen this kind of delay before in Saudi Arabia. We had been impressed and honored to see the privilege, courtesy and respect shown to representatives of Aramco at the ceremony in the square.

A few days later, we heard an amazing story of an incident that took place after we left Riyadh. As planned, all Muslim visitors proceeded to the mosque for prayers after the ceremony in the square. When prayers at the mosque were concluded, all the guests were excused and departed the scene, and the King's family proceeded to the burial site. However, Idi Amin insisted on going to the gravesite with the family, in defiance of normal practice. When they arrived at the burial ground, the Ugandan President further insisted on helping to dig the grave and personally wielded a shovel. No one, it seems, dared stop him.

In 1979, when Idi Amin was ousted from office in Uganda, Saudi Arabia offered him safe haven. He had obviously made a positive impression on the Saudi Government, which provided him with a home in Jeddah until his death there, at King Faisal Specialist Hospital, in August 2003. Saudi culture and custom, with their strong tradition of hospitality, stood fast in extending to the controversial leader medical assistance and asylum in time of urgent need.

We later learned that Petroleum Minister Yamani was standing beside the King when the assassination took place. He verified that the killer was a deranged nephew – his half-brother's son, Faisal ibn Musa'id.

King Faisal's passing was deeply mourned throughout the Kingdom, where he was highly respected as a strong and competent leader. He was noted for his personal ethics and his fairness, and was always considerate of the feelings and needs of his people.

Crown Prince Khalid ibn Abdulaziz was promptly named King and Prince Fahd ibn Abdulaziz became Crown Prince.

King Khalid was a personable and kind-hearted "man of the people." He ruled with little fanfare, and in general retained the same Cabinet and staff that Faisal had employed, maintaining the status quo in his policies. King Khalid loved the desert, where he often traveled and camped in his spare time. His hobby was falconry and he proudly collected the finest hunting birds.

I recall a discussion I had with King Khalid in December 1977, at a state dinner he hosted in Riyadh for visiting U.S. President Jimmy Carter. As these events go, this was a small affair, with 100 guests or fewer.

When I arrived along with the other guests in the anteroom of the dining area, we were greeted by King Khalid and in turn by President Carter. I stayed behind to chat a bit with the President, whom I had not met previously.

Soon one of the King's protocol officers approached me. He whispered to me that

King Khalid was now free, and suggested that I talk with him. The King told me he had two things he wanted to discuss with me.

First of all, he said that Aramco had a very good man whom I should pay attention to and treat well. "His name is John," the King said. He didn't know his last name. Since Aramco had many employees named John, I asked him where John worked. He replied: "Goodness, I don't know." The King had met him while hunting in the desert on several occasions; he said John spoke good Arabic and was interested in falconry as well. I promised to identify John and take note of him. The man turned out to be John E. Burchard Jr., who worked in our Arabic research and relations group. He was a talented and knowledgeable researcher, and one of the authors of Aramco's highly-regarded book Biotopes of the Western Arabian Gulf, a definitive study of the marine biology and ecology of the Saudi coast.[1]

Secondly, the King remarked that he wanted the evening's dinner to proceed well and properly, but he didn't want the President to make a speech or feel obliged to do so. He asked me for advice. I suggested that, as King and host, he might stand up promptly after he finished his meal and suggest that everyone return to the anteroom for coffee, and that he personally should lead the way. Once there, everyone would be standing, and neither the President nor anyone else would have an opportunity to deliver a speech.

He truly appreciated the suggestion and deftly followed my recommendation, bringing the dinner to a close without any speeches.

---

[1] Philip W. Basson, John E. Burchard Jr., John T. Hardy and Andrew R.G. Price, *Biotopes of the Western Arabian Gulf: Marine Life and Environments of Saudi Arabia. Dhahran, Saudi Arabia:* Aramco Dept. of Loss Prevention and Environmental Affairs, 1977.

*Sheikh Ahmed Zaki Yamani, Petroleum Minister of
Saudi Arabia. Photo by S.M. Amin.*

Chapter 20
The OPEC Hostage Crisis

During the week of December 13, 1975, the Saudi Petroleum Minister, Sheikh Ahmed Zaki Yamani, requested use of an Aramco Gulfstream II business jet so that he could meet a tight official schedule in Europe during the busy pre-Christmas season. Winter weather can be severe in Europe and Christmas is a joyous but hectic travel time for visitors.

The OPEC oil ministers were meeting at the organization's Vienna headquarters on Sunday, December 21, and Yamani needed to be in London the following Monday or Tuesday for a speaking engagement at an important international gathering. The Aramco jet was available, so we readily agreed and assigned a crew along with one of our best captains, who had flown the Minister a number of times before. The crew would remain in Vienna with the plane, ready to take Yamani on the next leg of his trip as required.

The Gulfstream II, a 14-passenger long-range corporate jet, left Saudi Arabia on Saturday, delivering Yamani and his aides in Vienna the same day. The plane and crew overnighted in the Austrian capital and stood by to leave on Sunday or Monday, depending on developments at the OPEC meeting.

Late Sunday afternoon, at my Dhahran office, I received an urgent call from our jet's captain in Vienna. A frightening situation was developing in Vienna. A terrorist group, he said, had stormed OPEC headquarters and taken a number of ministers and staff hostage. The terrorists had demanded that Austria supply an aircraft to fly them and their hostages out of the country. Apparently they had threatened to begin killing captives if the Austrians failed to comply with their demands. The Austrian authorities had yielded, and had prepared a DC-9 aircraft and crew to transport the terrorists and their OPEC captives to a country on the southern Mediterranean coast.

When I asked the captain where he had gotten his information, he said he and his co-pilot had listened to the tower, and the co-pilot had talked to the refuelers and the crew of the Austrian aircraft. He told me he had prepared our Gulfstream for take-off in the event that Yamani and his staff were released, so the plane could then make a quick departure with them aboard. He said he had parked our jet far enough away from the commandeered aircraft to be relatively unnoticed by anyone boarding the other plane.

After discussing options with the captain, I concluded we had two choices if Yamani was not released. The captain could return the Gulfstream to Dhahran after waiting a reasonable interval, or he could tail the hijacked Austrian plane – inconspicuously, at a discreet distance, listening to their communications with the target air terminal – and if possible land behind them later and wait to follow them further if necessary. The terrorists would no doubt be having ongoing radio discussions with their destination country. Our Gulfstream crew might be able to monitor these conversations and determine whether to continue tailing the Austrian plane.

The captain and I agreed he would do everything in his power to avoid being identified by the destination airport as having any relationship with the Austrian DC-9. If he had any doubts or concerns, he should refuel and depart immediately for Europe. I didn't want the pilot and co-pilot to face any unforeseen dangers, or have their motives questioned as to their reasons for landing.

By Sunday afternoon, the world's news media were reporting the capture of the OPEC ministers and their aides in Vienna. The reports said 50 or more OPEC ministers and staff had been seized on Saturday by a six-member commando unit led by the international terrorist known as Carlos "the Jackal."[1] Shortly after seizing OPEC headquarters, Carlos began negotiating with the Austrian government. He demanded that a communiqué in support of the Palestinian cause be read on Austrian radio and television every two hours. He threatened to kill his hostages if the plane was not ready by Sunday morning.

Meanwhile, all the hostages – according to Vienna Police, as many as 96 persons, including Austrian staff – spent a terrified night locked in a large auditorium with the terrorists, who repeatedly threatened to kill them the next morning. Yamani himself is quoted in his biography as saying that he began arguing with Carlos, who told him that he was his prime hostage.[2] I recall Yamani telling us later that one phrase Carlos constantly used in his conversations with the Saudi Minister was: "You are my superstar."

By approximately 5 a.m. Monday morning, the Austrian plane was ready to depart. The terrorists released about half of their hostages – those who were residents of Vienna and other lower-level employees. Carlos and his commandos then took the remaining OPEC ministers and staff – a total of about 40 hostages – and loaded them on the DC-9, which departed for Tripoli, Libya, at 7 a.m. The flight was expected to take some three hours. But soon after departure, the terrorists changed their destination to Algiers.

After phoning me and confirming our plans, the captain of the Aramco Gulfstream also departed a short time later, maintaining a discreet distance that allowed for some monitoring of the DC-9.

The Austrian DC-9 landed in Algiers. After about five hours of negotiations with Algerian authorities, Carlos released all of the non-Arab hostages except for the Iranian OPEC representative, Jamshid Amouzegar (who was later Prime Minister under the Shah). This left 20 hostages on board, including six Arab ministers, when the plane left, once more destined for Tripoli. Upon arrival in Libya, Carlos attempted unsuccessfully to negotiate for a longer-range aircraft that could fly them on to Baghdad. Finally, after

---

[1] Carlos' real name was Ilich Ramírez Sánchez. Born in Venezuela in 1949, he was a member of the Popular Front for the Liberation of Palestine (PFLP), the organization that reportedly planned the attack on OPEC headquarters.

[2] Jeffrey Robinson, *Yamani: The Inside Story*. London: Simon & Schuster, 1988.

midnight on Tuesday morning, the terrorists decided to return to Algiers, where they planned to negotiate for a larger plane. But before they left Tripoli, Carlos released the Libyan and Algerian oil ministers and eight other hostages, including two lower-level members of the Saudi delegation. Khader Herzallah, Yamani's close aide, was not released in Tripoli, and continued on with the Minister.

This left four oil ministers still on board the DC-9 – Amouzegar of Iran, Abdul Muttaleb Al Kazemi of Kuwait, Iraq's Tayeh Abdul Karim and Yamani. En route to Algiers after dark, Carlos unexpectedly sought permission to land in Tunis. Tunisian authorities would have none of this – they prevented the DC-9 from landing by turning off all the runway lights.

So the Austrian plane continued on and landed once more in Algiers, where Carlos got off the plane. After a long time – presumably involving meetings with Algerian officials – the terrorist leader returned. Carlos began cursing Yamani and Amouzegar for the longest time; then he left the plane with his fellow terrorists for the last time.[3] The hostages were allowed to disembark at 5:45 a.m. At last, they were free. Yamani told me later – and this is confirmed in his biography – that Carlos's right-hand man, a Palestinian named Khalid, had told the Saudi Minister: "You will be killed much sooner than you expect. Carlos will never let you live."

Upon leaving the Austrian DC-9, Yamani immediately rushed across the tarmac to the waiting Aramco plane, which took off for Switzerland, where he was met by his wife, Tammam, and two of his children. He then reboarded the Gulfstream and flew to Amman, where King Khalid, who was on an official visit to Jordan at the time, welcomed his Petroleum Minister and congratulated him on his safety. The Minister then flew back to Jeddah, where he received a hero's welcome.

From that point on, the Saudi Government provided Yamani with 24-hour protection by British bodyguards, who traveled with him at all times.

As for Carlos, he was finally apprehended in Sudan in 1994 and extradited to France, where he is currently serving a life sentence for the murder of two French counter-intelligence agents and a French government informant. It was widely reported that Libya's Col. Qaddafi was behind the Vienna hostage crisis and probably financed it. The full story behind the attack may never be known.

---

[3] Robinson, *ibid.*, p. 169.

Chapter 21
Powering the East: SCECO Is Born

One of the most pressing needs in Saudi Arabia's Eastern Province during the early to mid-1970s was a solution to the area's electric power problems. The power utilities of the province were primitive and lacked a consolidated grid. By contrast, Aramco had its own efficient, modern electrical network, designed to assure the smooth operation of its oil business, and at times this successful system proved to be somewhat embarrassing.

Aramco's power system served its producing plants, refineries, tanker loading facilities and storage areas. We also supplied electricity to four large, fully-equipped communities for Western employees and higher-level Saudi employees. In addition, we brought the employee home ownership communities into our electricity supply program.

Aramco's electric power was as reliable as you could find anywhere in the world. When we visited local towns in the Eastern Province, usually at night for dinner at a restaurant, we would sometimes experience frustrating power outages. In summer it was extremely hot, and air conditioning was crucial. From these towns you could stare out into the darkness during the outages and see Aramco communities in the distance, all lit up with their power plants still functioning. This state of affairs could only result in public discontent, as people began wondering why only Aramco's foreigners and its "elite" Saudi employees had reliable electric power.

I was convinced that we had to do something about the local electric power utilities. These small, privately-owned companies were working with old, outdated diesel generating sets hooked to rudimentary transmission networks. Their equipment and lines were woefully inadequate for the growing local communities of the Eastern Province. What they needed was a modern, centralized power grid that would serve all local communities and support growing business requirements. The domestic electrical power networks needed to be as efficient and reliable as the company's own grid.

I thought a good start might be to expand the Aramco power system into nearby towns – admittedly a very expensive proposition. Our strategy, I felt, should be to convince the Saudi Government to buy up the local electrical companies and supply funds to expand the Aramco facilities, and then systematically rebuild the local distribution system. I brought the idea to our shareholder directors, telling them this would be a good way to tie the local communities and Aramco together. It would also encourage the Government and public to view Aramco as a national asset.

At the same time, we were engaged in early discussions with the Saudi Government about a major nationwide gas utilization program – what would come to be known as the Kingdom's Master Gas System. The Government wanted Aramco to design, build and operate a gas gathering and processing system that would fuel petrochemical and other plants in the twin industrial cities of Jubail on the east coast and Yanbu' on the west. During these preliminary talks, we had some concerns about how Aramco's own electric power needs would be affected under various versions of the gas program.

The four shareholders were reluctant to proceed with an electric power scheme for the Eastern Province, declaring that with the Master Gas System on the horizon, two projects of this magnitude might be too much for Aramco to handle at the same time. In two stormy Board discussions, most of the directors were almost vehemently opposed to expanding our electric power capacity to the public.

But we – Aramco's management – argued that the Master Gas System itself would require a major power expansion, and we wanted to enhance the company's image in the Eastern Province rather than see it damaged. These arguments finally carried the day. The directors reluctantly agreed that I could raise the idea at an appropriate level of Government and see how Saudi officials might react.

As it developed, I finally went to see the Minister of the Interior, who was Crown Prince (and later King) Fahd ibn Abdulaziz. I knew him well enough to explore a few ideas with him. I told him my thoughts about the local electric power systems

Frank Jungers at table with King Fahd and Clifford Garvin, the CEO and Chairman of Exxon (far left).

in the Eastern Province, and said that I felt they should be tied into a common grid. I explained to him that there were really three main problems.

The first was that the various power companies in the local towns would need to be bought out. I felt this was a task that Aramco should not attempt – rather, the Government should take the appropriate steps to deal with the local electric companies, buying them out one by one. I also said we should form a Saudi company that would include the existing Aramco power system along with the new local power systems and the expansion they required. This power utility would belong to the Saudi Government, but Aramco would operate it and manage it as though it were an Aramco company, for the benefit of the Government. Aramco operation of the new company was mandatory, since all of our oil operations relied on electricity, and ultimately the country's total income was at stake and depended upon our performance.

Prince Fahd immediately asked what we would do for the rest of the country. I said that eventually all the country's electric companies could perhaps be tied together, but for now we should start in the Eastern Province, because that was where Aramco's power facilities were.

"You could transmit power to Riyadh," the Prince said suddenly.

I agreed that this was technically possible, but I suggested we start small and get the company going first in the Eastern Province.

Prince Fahd smiled and said, "I want it in Riyadh. Why don't you do it now?"

I jokingly told him that I didn't want powerful people like him calling me up in the middle of the night complaining that the air conditioning was out. We both laughed, and Fahd said with a smile, "Of course, I would never do anything like that!"

So in August 1976, after much preparation by Aramco and the Government, King Khalid issued a Royal Decree creating the Saudi Consolidated Electric Company (SCECO), which unified 26 local electric companies and Aramco's power system.

Aramco organized and operated SCECO, contributing its operating organization and expertise. The electric system expanded rapidly in the Eastern Province to include even small towns receiving power for the first time.[1] The four Aramco shareholders

---

[1] The SCECO blueprint was later extended throughout the Kingdom and by 2000 all power generation facilities were connected to the power grid of the newly-formed national entity, the Saudi Electricity Company (SEC).

came to recognize the merit of SCECO for Aramco and themselves. It is not fair to say they were "disappointed" with the outcome, but they had hoped that this development would not have moved so quickly (in fact, it took a number of months). However, as the SCECO project progressed, it became clear it was a "win-win" – the local population was glad to have the new electric company, which pulled together all the local grids of the Eastern Province and created a new level of efficiency and service. As some Saudis put it, "By God, Aramco did a good job!"

At the same time, the Saudi Government got credit for having directed Aramco to carry out the consolidation project – which, of course, had come about as the result of a Royal Decree. Today, Saudi Arabia has a national power grid run by SCECO's nationwide successor, the Saudi Electricity Company (SEC). Aramco's original concept, though, is still in place, and the Kingdom has a reliable power system as a result. At the same time, Aramco continues to operate its own electric power utilities to main its operations throughout the Kingdom.

Despite the growing workload of the gas expansion project, Aramco moved promptly to staff the new power company with the necessary management. SCECO needed an effective management team ready to go on Day One, and the best way to assure this was to draw on the proven technical and administrative skills of Aramco's oil operations management. It was Aramco's largest major effort to develop and supply a solution to a critical public need.

Redesigning and repurposing facilities and services for customer use outside the Aramco fence required an array of skills beyond the technical and engineering expertise for which our company was so well known. Organizational management expertise, bolstered by strong people skills, was needed to merge 26 small, poorly-functioning companies into the Aramco grid, and thereby provide reliable, safe power into thousands of homes – even into remote villages where no electric power had existed before.

One of the most notable talents in this effort was Abdallah S. Jum'ah, then a creative Aramco executive on the rise, with a government relations and public relations background. Jum'ah was assigned on loan to SCECO as manager of Power Systems Public and Customer Affairs.[2]

---

[2] From 1981 to 1984, Abdallah Jum'ah served as managing director of SCECO East and concurrently as vice president of Power Systems at Aramco.

The Royal Decree creating SCECO caused great excitement and anticipation in the Eastern Province. Even though Aramco and SCECO were moving forward rapidly, time was needed to design and construct the grid, including months to import the required power equipment. Jum'ah listened patiently to the villagers' concerns and explained to them why building the facilities and connecting their villages to the grid could not happen overnight. He once related a story illustrating the kind of knowledge and culture gaps he dealt with regularly in the course of his assignment – gaps that it was his responsibility to close.

SCECO was running power to a line of ten villages, and needed to build a substation to drop the voltage of the main line for village use. A discussion ensued among SCECO representatives on site as to where to place the substation, and it was suggested that, for value engineering purposes, it be placed near the next-to-last village, so that a cheaper line could be run to the final village. This conversation was overheard by Bedouins from the last village, who sent a delegation to Jum'ah, saying that they would not settle for "leftovers" – they felt that the power coming in on a cheaper line would be "leftover" electricity, not quite as good as the current running through the main line.

Abdallah Jum'ah later remarked: "I've seen hundreds of people in my office, from all walks of life – someone concerned about a problem or a representative from a village asking about progress on the distribution network. I loved dealing with people and it's been the most rewarding experience of my career so far."[3]

Jum'ah's accomplishments at SCECO were a key part of the solid career record that led to his later appointment as president and CEO of Saudi Aramco, from 1995 to 2008.

---

[3] Scott McMurray, *Energy to the World: The Story of Saudi Aramco.* Houston: Aramco Services Company, 2011, Vol. 2, p. 62.

Chapter 22
Master Gas Plan

Prior to the 1960s, when flying over the Middle East oil fields at night, you could see a vast, glowing panorama of oilfield flares, ranging from Iraq through Iran and down the Arabian Gulf shoreline of Kuwait, Saudi Arabia, Bahrain and the Emirates. In Saudi Arabia, production was increasing rapidly from high-pressure fields that were producing hundreds and even thousands of barrels of oil per day without the help of pumps at the wells. This is dramatically different from the United States today, where most wells are pumped and cannot produce much more than 10 to 15 barrels per day. Yes, only 10 to 15!

When oil is produced under pressure, varying amounts of gases are released from the liquid petroleum in much the same way that the fizz leaves a bottle of Coke when you remove the cap. The gas released from the oil consists mostly of butane, propane and methane.[1] In the case of Middle East production, these gases had little market value in the world at that time. Since most of these gases also contained hydrogen sulfide (H2S), a very poisonous and corrosive chemical compound known for its "rotten egg" smell, for safety reasons they needed to be burned off by flaring. Flaring is normally done from a vertical flare stack that rises high above ground level, but the process may involve potential health hazards, and today it is known to add to worldwide emissions of carbon dioxide.

Three oil workers pose with flare in the background in Abqaiq, 1975. Photo by Dorothy Miller.

Beginning in the early 1960s, Aramco injected a small amount of produced associated gas back into the earth to repressurize certain fields. Some of the propane and butane was processed and stored under pressure for local industrial use. In that form it was known as natural gas liquids or NGL.

----

[1] Gas released from produced crude oil is called associated gas. Methane (CH_4) is the main component of natural gas.

The Saudi Government purchased Aramco's local gas liquids business and set up the state-run company Petromin to develop the gas products market in the Kingdom. Here again, we see a familiar pattern, as Aramco and the Government, growing in tandem, worked together to develop what would eventually prove to be an important local market. This market continued to grow, but it was too small to absorb all of Aramco's ever-increasing production.

Aramco management knew the company could not keep flaring gas forever.

Flares in Abqaiq, 1971. Photo by Dorothy Miller.

Environmentally, it was a net negative, due to possible release of methane, H_2S, aromatic hydrocarbons and other substances. In addition, everyone recognized that associated gas was a potentially valuable resource, for which markets should be found. Gas usage was growing to some extent in the domestic economy, and the company would use as much gas as possible to repressurize fields. The four Aramco shareholder companies began to develop the Japanese market, which was using more NGL for power generation and as a fuel for trucks and cars. In a relatively short period, NGL sales to Japan reached 600,000 barrels per day. With the propane and butane being sold in the Far East, this left the methane or natural gas, which could be used for electric power generation in Saudi Arabia – but our projections showed that the Kingdom's power generation requirements would quickly outgrow Aramco's existing production.

Early in the 1970s, due to the increase in oil prices, the Kingdom's revenues from petroleum were reaching new heights – with Aramco, of course, providing over 90 percent of them. Flush with funds for national investment, the Saudi Government decided to engage the Stanford Research Institute to chart a five-year plan for developing the infrastructure of the country. [2]

The goal of the plan was to spur further industrialization in the country by diversifying the economy – and expanding employment opportunities for a sharply increasing number of young Saudi jobseekers, many of whom would be equipped with college degrees. The largest and most obvious resource for these endeavors was the associated gas being produced along with the crude oil.

In 1974, the Government asked Petromin, which had taken over distribution of NGL within the Kingdom, to do a feasibility study on future uses for Aramco's associated natural gas. Petromin contracted with Texas Eastern Engineering Company, a subsidiary of a large U.S. natural gas transmission company, to prepare a feasibility study on how the Stanford Research infrastructure proposals could be implemented using Aramco gas. The Texas Eastern study, completed in 1975, showed that huge projected needs in the domestic economy would require continual and ongoing growth in Aramco.

The Petroleum Ministry gave the study to Aramco, and we were asked to develop a plan and schedule for implementing domestic gas utilization, complete with financial estimates. The Government assumed that Aramco would undertake this huge project because it had to be coordinated with oil operations. After review in Aramco, we realized that what was envisioned amounted to the most ambitious energy project in history.

Before this, in the early 1970s, as worldwide demand for oil increased, Aramco

---

[2] Founded by Stanford University in 1946, SRI International, as it is now called, has been a non-profit independent institute since 1970, conducting client-sponsored research and development for government agencies, commercial businesses, foundations and other organizations.

had begun expanding its workforce, which reached a total of 19,500 employees by 1975. This expansion had in turn triggered major growth in our training programs.

Two big energy projects had caused this expansion. The Zuluf Field in the Arabian Gulf – one of the Kingdom's largest offshore fields, sometimes described as a "super-giant" – was a unique development brought onstream in 1973.[3] In 1959, Aramco had built a gas–oil separation plant (GOSP) offshore to separate the gas from crude oil produced at Safaniya, the world's largest offshore field, but only handling the first stage of separation. In the case of Zuluf, we had moved the entire gas–oil separation process offshore. Crude oil from Zuluf wells flowed to an offshore plant mounted on piles above the waters of the Gulf, where the gas was removed. The crude oil was then sent on through underwater lines to a rather remarkable 1.8-million-barrel "floating

King Khalid cuts the ribbon to officially inaugurate Berri NGL plant, part of Master Gas System.

---

[3] Zuluf, discovered in 1965, lies in the northern part of offshore Saudi Arabia, near the Safaniya and Marjan fields.

storage tank." The floating storage tank was actually a stationary oil tanker named the F. A. Davies (after Aramco's late chairman). After it was loaded, the oil was pumped to seagoing tankers for export.

Even more unique was the huge Qurayyah Sea Water Treatment Plant, built to pump clean, treated water from the Arabian Gulf into injection wells surrounding the major onshore oil reservoirs of the Eastern Province. Design work on Qurayyah began in 1974 and the facility began operations in 1978. Seawater injection was designed to maintain production pressures and production rates. It also reduced the need for gas injection, freeing up associated gas for industrial use. The original water injection rate of Qurayyah was approximately 4.5 million barrels per day. Capacity expansion related to the Master Gas Plan and other programs have meant that Qurayyah is now injecting more than 12 million barrels of treated seawater per day to underlay Saudi Aramco's major reservoirs to maintain reservoir pressures and insure maximum production of the reservoir.

With all this activity in the 1970s, and amid Aramco's Government-mandated creation of the Saudi Consolidated Electric Company and the transmission grid for the Eastern Province, along came yet another massive engineering and construction effort – the Master Gas Plan.

This latest development meant that Aramco needed to accelerate and extend even further the education and training of its highest-potential employees, and pursue intensive management development of those with high executive capabilities.

The Saudi Government's five-year development plan was updated in February 1975 to include the Master Gas Plan, a project unprecedented in scope as well as cost. Specifically, Aramco was asked to design, develop and operate a gas gathering and processing system to fuel a Kingdom-wide industrial network that was being developed on a parallel track. Approval of this plan marked one of the last major acts of King Faisal before his assassination.

After conducting its own studies, Aramco estimated the Kingdom's Master Gas System (MGS) would cost up to $14 billion. (Converting this estimate to today's prices, the figure is in the neighborhood of $35–$40 billion.) The American shareholder companies were somewhat divided about whether Aramco should take part in this program. From their perspective, there was little profit in selling Saudi natural gas. Committing Aramco to the MGS was a distraction they felt might impinge upon and divert Aramco's resources from an already booming oil business.

As Aramco's CEO, I advocated a different view. I thought the gas initiative would be a new vehicle for making Aramco and its American shareholders and management increasingly important and relevant to the Kingdom's development. Some of our employees believed (with some justification) that I was not about to let an outside company elbow its way into the Kingdom and run the gas program if Aramco could do anything to prevent it. This may have been partially true, but I also felt that in any case we needed to recognize the environmental harm of continued massive flaring of associated gas. Aramco and the oil industry could not long sustain the negative impact of this reality on their reputations and brands. Finally the shareholders acquiesced, especially since the Saudi Government had decided to pay for the project from its own revenues – and not from Aramco profits.

The MGS was designed overall to provide fuel and feedstock for domestic electric power, for desalination plants and for petrochemical, fertilizer and steelmaking facilities. Two of the largest proposed users of gas were the sprawling industrial cities being constructed at Yanbu' on the Red Sea and Jubail on the Arabian Gulf. Aramco would also use the gas to power many of its own facilities. At the heart of the system therefore were gas-gathering facilities in four oilfields of the Eastern Province and gas processing plants both in the Eastern Province and on the Red Sea coast, along with export terminals at Ras Tanura, Jubail and Yanbu'. By the time the initial system was completed in 1982, it would process the energy equivalent of about 750,000 barrels of crude oil a day.

As part of the MGS, the company's existing oilfield pressure maintenance systems were essentially replaced. To maintain oilfield reservoirs and pressures, the company had previously relied on injections of associated gas and of water from onshore saline aquifers. Both of these methods were replaced by injection of treated Gulf seawater from Qurayyah. The Master Gas Program contained enough capital to provide for huge expansion of seawater injection facilities and also to provide an 800-mile pipeline, known as the East–West NGL Pipeline, to be built across the Arabian Peninsula and over the mountains of the Hejaz, to deliver NGL to the Red Sea industrial areas.

To support MGS construction and various oil expansion projects, Aramco scrambled to build and operate construction-worker camps at eight sites in the Eastern Province by 1977. The camps could house as many as 37,900 bachelors and 875 families. When it could not find or build sites fast enough on land, the company had five-story accommodation barges towed in from Singapore and Japan, each with its own generators, desalination facilities, air conditioning, dining halls and recreation areas. These "floating hotels," as they were called, were anchored offshore near Dhahran and housed about 4,500 workers.

The MGS had a dramatic impact on Saudi contractors and contributed greatly to the growth of a wide range of local industries and businesses, such as earth-moving, construction, steel, cement and welding. In 1975, Aramco awarded Saudi firms contracts for MGS work valued at $250 million. The following year, the total jumped to $1.7 billion. In 1977, the value of some 730 contracts with Saudi firms reached nearly $2 billion. Much of this activity occurred in the Eastern Province; similar business expansion – though not quite as extensive – also occurred on the Rea Sea coast, where the gas system connected via the East–West Pipeline with petrochemical and other plants in Yanbu's industrial city.

Chapter 23
Royal Succession

Americans and other Westerners often ask me "How long will the Saudi monarchy last?" and "Why don't the Saudis discontinue the monarchy and replace it with a democratic form of government?" Usually the questioners are unfamiliar with Middle East societies and politics. They are also unaware of the history of the Saudi monarchy and its differences from other monarchies, both past and present.

My answer normally begins with the observation that, as history tells us, absolute monarchy is for the most part a political system of the past, and many of the world's surviving kingdoms are constitutional or token monarchies, with real power residing in a representative, elected government. However, the Saudi monarchy is quite unique in two distinct respects.

First, Saudi Arabia is the home of the sacred sites of a leading world religion and as such is held responsible for protecting these shrines and making them available for visits by millions of Muslim pilgrims, both during the annual Hajj season and throughout the year. In other words, Saudi Arabia is the headquarters of Islam.

Saudi Arabia's current political system was established in 1932 by the head of the House of Saud, Abdulaziz Al Saud, after subduing rival tribes and unifying most of the Arabian Peninsula – with the exception of some coastal areas that today make up the independent states of Kuwait, the United Arab Emirates, Qatar, Oman and Yemen. The western region of the Kingdom, known as the Hejaz, contains the holy cities of Mecca and Medina, the historic port and traditional commercial and diplomatic capital of Jeddah, as well as Taif, the summer capital in the mountains above Jeddah, where the government moves each year to avoid the stifling heat and humidity of summer.

In unifying the Kingdom, Abdulaziz minimized military operations in the western region that might have posed dangers to the Holy Places. Nonetheless, in the spring of 1924, Abdulaziz – then known as King of the Najd – sent a military force that took control of the cities of Taif and Mecca, with the King cautioning his people not to cause unnecessary damage to the cities or Holy Places. As a result of the quick takeover, the existing leader of the Hejaz, Sharif Hussein ibn Ali, fled to Jeddah, where he set up his defenses. On March 5, 1924, two days after the Turkish government abolished the traditional Caliphate, Sharif Hussein suddenly and spontaneously declared himself Caliph of all Muslims. The Caliph was viewed as successor of the Prophet Muhammad and at least spiritual (sometimes temporal) leader of the Islamic community worldwide.

Abdulaziz knew he would soon have to travel from the Riyadh area in the Najd to Mecca in the Hejaz to take charge of rapidly-changing events. But before moving, he felt he had to communicate with the Muslim world to explain the situation concerning Sharif Hussein's unexpected declaration of himself as Caliph (and thus head of the Holy Places), a move that had enraged millions of the world's Muslims.

While I do not pretend to be a historian or an expert on Muslim thinking, it seems clear to me that King Abdulaziz was very sensitive to world Muslim opinion when he opted not to take over the Hejaz region without demonstrating to all Muslims that he could and would protect the Holy Places. The global Islamic community needed to feel confident that Abdulaziz was making it possible for Muslims of all nationalities to perform the Hajj as safely and as comfortably as possible.

To reassure Muslims, he issued "a solemn statement for circulation throughout the whole Islamic World" in which he declared that his sole purpose of entering the

Hejaz was to guarantee the freedom of pilgrimage and to evict the false Caliph and his family. Abdulaziz further stated he had no intention of annexing or dominating the Holy Cities of Mecca and Medina.[1]

After that declaration in November 1924, he set out for Mecca by camel, moving slowly through the villages along the way, where people came out to meet him and pledge their loyalty. When he reached the gates of Mecca he unbuckled his sword, took off his red-and-white *shemagh* headdress, donned the white robes of a pilgrim and entered the city bareheaded and in total humility, performing the obligations of a pilgrim.

Abdulaziz reopened all Red Sea ports used by foreign pilgrims and re-established order in the area. In June 1926, before the annual Hajj, he invited leaders of all Muslim countries to a congress in Mecca to discuss the future government of the Holy Places. Sixty-nine world leaders attended. By the end of the conference, all had accepted the new reality that from then on King Abdulaziz and his Government would control and protect Islam's Holy Places. That year, more people made the Hajj pilgrimage than ever before.

Over the years since then, the Saudi monarchy has given serious attention and focus to its role as representative of the world's Muslim communities, particularly in the context of the Hajj, which is a requirement of the faith. The significance of this role should not be underestimated.

In the Western world, it is sometimes argued that the kings of Saudi Arabia have given too much authority to the conservative Wahhabi religious movement and thus have not moved quickly enough in liberalizing Saudi society, expanding women's rights and allowing for changes in various other aspects of lifestyle.[2]

By and large, non-Muslims fail to understand that the King of Saudi Arabia is also "Custodian of the Holy Places" of Islam – an attribute formally designated as part of

---

[1] Michael Darlow and Barbara Bray, *Ibn Saud: The Desert Warrior and His Legacy.* London: Quartet Books, 2010, p. 302.

[2] Wahhabism is the popular term for a fundamentalist (and revivalist) movement in Saudi Arabia founded in the 18th century by theologian Mohammed ibn Abdul Wahhab of Najd. Abdul Wahhab and his family, the Al ash-Sheikhs, forged a close alliance with the Al Saud clan that survives to this day. The Wahhabis call themselves Muwahhidun, or Unitarians, with belief in the one God serving as the centerpiece of their theology.

his royal title since the reign of King Fahd. The King is regarded as protector of these holy sites by all faithful Muslims. It is a part of their faith to make the pilgrimage to Mecca and Medina at least once in their lives, if they have the means. Thus it is incumbent upon the King to remain conscious of the expectations of the Muslim umma or community, not only in Saudi Arabia but also internationally – particularly in countries with large Muslim populations, such as Indonesia, Pakistan, India, Bangladesh and China.

Certainly this qualification has to be of concern to those who decide on the succession of kings in Saudi Arabia.

The second unique aspect of the Saudi monarchy is that it represents, in a unique and distinctive way, the many textures and colors of the national fabric in Saudi Arabia. The monarchy created by Abdulaziz became, over time, what I would call a "representational monarchy." During the years that Abdulaziz was pacifying and unifying the tribes, he married women in many key tribes, clans and families, doing so in full accordance with Sharia law and Islamic tradition.[3] These marriages gave the tribes and indeed all Saudis a political, economic and social stake in the future nation. The sons of the King's marriages, as they grew to maturity, became significant leaders of their families. King Abdulaziz had a total of more than 40 sons from these marriages, most of whom could and did hold high-level positions in the Government. Their ages, of course, were spread out over quite a number of years.

After the death of King Abdulaziz, his eldest son, Prince Saud, became King. Saud had been named Crown Prince by his father, so his succession was expected. From then on, subsequent kings were also sons of Abdulaziz. Some sons who might have been candidates for kingship by virtue of their age were bypassed for various reasons. But in every case, a Crown Prince was named prior to the passing of the current King.

At Aramco, in the early days, we surmised that there was a system or procedure that was followed in selecting a new King from among the sons of Abdulaziz, because we noted that some candidates were being bypassed for reasons not apparent to us or the outside world.

We had also noticed that certain elders seemed to be influential at the King's

---

[3] Islam traditionally allows men to have up to four wives at any given time, on the condition that all wives are treated equally.

The Shrine at Mecca taken by Shaikh Amin in 1977. The area around the shrine has been greatly enlarged to accommodate tremendously larger crowds of pilgrims arriving these days In the Sacred Mosque of Mecca, Muslim pilgrims perform the tawaf, *circling the Ka'aba or God's House in one of the rituals of the Hajj or pilgrimage. Each Hajj season, millions of pilgrims, most of them non-Saudi, converge on the Holy City. World Muslim opinion plays an unofficial but necessary role in the selection of Saudi kings, whose responsibilities include protection of the holy sites in Mecca and Medina. Photo by S.M. Amin.*

regular Thursday morning *majlis*, or open meeting, when the people of the Kingdom were invited to meet the monarch and petition him for relief and other types of support.

King Abdulaziz had created a system that utilized his sons (to each other they were often half-brothers) as channels of communication between average citizens and the King and his Government. This system enabled him to pull together a somewhat fractious tribal society and in so doing create a nation of men and women who were proud to call themselves Saudis. In traditional Saudi tribal society, the elders of the tribe – its natural leaders – were looked to for advice and important decisions involving the group. The sons of Abdulaziz had been raised in this society, and as young men had looked up to tribal elders. Now, as they grew older, these brothers and half-brothers often found themselves in the roles of elders whose counsel was highly valued and much sought after.

At Aramco, we sometimes tried to guess which elders – sons of Abdulaziz and others – were the most respected advisors in the King's inner circle. We had no inside knowledge about how successors to the throne were chosen. But it made sense to us that the process involved consultations with key senior individuals, including not only the sons of Abdulaziz and but also other important personalities in Saudi society.

One such figure most certainly was Sheikh Abdullah ibn Abdul Rahman, younger brother of King Abdulaziz, who was seen frequently at the King's *majlis*. In the early 1950s, as a young engineer, I was once assigned to travel with an electrician to the palace of Sheikh Abdullah in Riyadh. The company had been asked to devise an air conditioning system for this well-built (and ecologically sustainable) traditional mud structure. I made three road trips from Dhahran to Riyadh. In those days the trip took about 10 hours by car, mostly across sand and unpaved road. We eventually installed a number of powerful air conditioning window units in the palace that did the job. While we were there, Sheikh Abdullah, who spoke limited English, and I, who at the time knew even less Arabic, would talk. He was a very inquisitive man, anxious to understand the basics of oil production, drilling techniques, exploration and the like.

I explained to him that oil exists in rock, and that when the pressure is released, it flows. He was surprised at such explanations, but nonetheless had the intelligence to ask the right sort of questions, because he had concluded that he lacked the necessary information to draw proper conclusions about the petroleum industry. And so we became friends, although he was older and almost like an uncle to me. Privately, in our company notes, Sheikh Abdullah was referred to affectionately as "Uncle Abby."

Years later, I went to see King Faisal in Taif, the summer capital. It was my first visit to the King after my appointment as chairman of Aramco. It was a Thursday morning, and King Faisal was conducting his usual *majlis*. In between his discussions with courtiers and petitioners, he and I would exchange pleasantries and talk about various matters. All of a sudden, the King grabbed my arm and said, "Abdullah is coming!" People at the other end of the *majlis* were beginning to stand, and the King also stood – as did I. Someone was walking toward us across the expansive floor, his sandals slapping softly – a short man with a gray beard and a pleasant face. He was looking directly at me.

"He has come to see you," King Faisal said. Yes, it was Sheikh Abdullah, and he had come to congratulate me on my new appointment. He sat down between the King and me, and we spent a brief but very pleasant time recalling incidents from our past. This experience, if nothing else, convinced me that certainly Sheikh Abdullah ibn Abdul Rahman had to be one member of that group of insiders who were present when heirs to the throne were selected.

King Fahd formally enshrined the rules of succession into Saudi Basic Law through a Royal Decree issued on March 1, 1992. In this decree, the King reaffirmed that "Saudi Arabia is a monarchy" and that "the throne is reserved to the sons and grandsons of the founder King Abdulaziz." The decree further stated that the "best among [these] would be named King by acclamation based on the Holy Book and the teachings of his Blessed Messenger."

Crown Prince Abdullah ibn Abdulaziz succeeded King Fahd in 2005, and little more than a year later, on October 20, 2006, the new King set up a special body called the Allegiance Commission to deal with the selection of royal successors and related organizational matters. A year later, the Government issued a series of detailed bylaws that provided for succession of the Crown Prince not only by the sons of King Abdulaziz but also by his grandsons.

The 35 members of the commission – consisting of 16 sons and 19 grandsons of King Abdulaziz – were then chosen in accordance with the law. In fact, the commission has already performed its function twice, following the untimely deaths of Crown Prince Sultan ibn Abdulaziz (in 2011) and Crown Prince Nayef ibn Abdulaziz (in 2012). Its recommendation after Prince Nayef's passing led to the appointment of Prince Salman ibn Abdulaziz as Crown Prince.

In summary, the Saudi monarchy is indeed unique because it continues to inspire confidence among Muslims worldwide as protector of the Holy Places and has a long record of accommodating and caring for the millions of pilgrims who come to the Kingdom each year in ever-increasing numbers to make the Hajj. The pilgrimage is a massive, costly undertaking that requires constant attention and commitment.

In addition, given the ruling family's ties through marriage to all the major tribes and families of Saudi Arabia, and its long-standing practice of constant consultation with these connected groups, the Saudi monarchy is uniquely representational, perhaps more so than any comparable government today, which makes for better stability.

Chapter 24
Environment Matters

My intention in this chapter is not to catalogue all of the major environmental activities of Aramco and the Saudi Government over the years, but rather to show that protecting the environment has, from the company's earliest times, always been a very important priority as we contributed to developing the country's infrastructure and industry. Our long-standing concern for the environment may come as a surprise to some, but keep in mind that Aramco from its earliest days was home to its first American expatriate workers and management. We were raising our families in Saudi Arabia, where our operations were being conducted, and the health and safety of our spouses and children were naturally of vital importance to us. The expanding Saudi workforce felt the same way about their own families, and thus the company consistently supported operations that protected the environment and health of everyone. The Saudi Government was quick to see the value in this approach, and it has been very active in developing and implementing sound environmental policies and programs.

I personally recall several important occasions that triggered comprehensive Aramco environmental policies as early as the 1950s, some of which came into play before they became recognized global issues.

Before the world became actively concerned about environmental protection issues, Aramco and its employees were taking notice of the possible environmental impact of major construction and oil shipping activity, especially around Ras Tanura, the company's refining center and the site of early port facilities that handled all oil tanker loadings and their movements offshore in the relatively pristine Arabian Gulf.

For about five years in the early 1950s, the community at Ras Tanura was home for my family and me – our very first home in Saudi Arabia. It was a very desirable location for all residents – for one thing, it had an outstanding white sand beach. The water was warm, and residents enjoyed recreational fishing and boating most of the year round.

In time, as tanker traffic grew, we noticed a growing number of tar-like globules and balls of oil washing up on the beaches and sticking to the feet of beachgoers. The company checked for possible leaks in the pipelines and the tanker loading equipment at the piers, but found no issues there. It was then that we realized that the oil tankers themselves were the problem. Tankers arriving to be loaded with crude oil cargoes were pumping out seawater ballast from their oily tanks prior to loading. This oily ballast was washing up on our beaches after the ships emptied their tanks to take on new oil cargoes. We decided to build pumping facilities and storage tanks onshore to recover and process the dirty ballast. We then required all arriving oil tankers to offload their ballast into Aramco's onshore tanks – after which Aramco removed the oily residue from the ballast water and safely disposed of the clean water.

Once Aramco had appropriate facilities in place, oil tankers that came in with empty ballast tanks were turned away and refused permission to load – clean ballast tanks meant that they had dumped dirty ballast into the sea while en route to Aramco's terminals. This tough new policy greatly reduced the pollution problems in the Gulf at an early stage – but not completely, because there were other ports in the Gulf that had not as yet adopted the Aramco system. However, in time they too began following the practice.

Kuwait oil fires set by Iraqi forces during 1990-91 Gulf War. Photo by Wendy Cocker.

All of a sudden, the roar ceased and the site was silent – a huge relief for all of us. The well had been brought under control by rough but logically sound methods that could only have been developed through extensive experience. None of this would have worked if Myron Kinley had not risked personal injury when the crane failed to set the tapered plug firmly into the blowing tubing. With oil spraying out around the taper and with the fire overhead, Kinley grabbed a sledgehammer and his shield. We both moved closer to the leak. Then he handed me his shield and leaped out on his gimpy leg to pound the plug down with a single blow of the sledgehammer. In my opinion, with that one blow he earned his entire fee.

Fortunately, thanks to Myron Kinley's skills and the dedication of Aramco's crews, the Fadhili fire was put out, the oil flow was stopped, and we were able to avoid an environmental crisis of wider proportions.

The Fadhili well fire prompted a complete review of the company's producing and drilling operations, especially with respect to potential security and safety problems faced by plants and wells in remote areas. In addition, all Aramco personnel were encouraged to spread the word to Saudi villagers and Bedouins of the potential dangers involved in entering oil installations.

Knowing the importance of the fishing and pearling industries to the people of the Arabian Gulf, Aramco decided to investigate what environmental risks might be encountered with our increasing marine activity. Not only were tanker and freighter activity on the rise, but Aramco had also discovered the world's largest offshore oilfield at Safaniya in the northern Gulf. Offshore drill rigs and production facilities could potentially become a source of contamination for coral reefs and disturb commercial and recreational fishing.

The offshore area between Bahrain Island and Saudi Arabia's Qatif oasis contained prolific oyster beds. Pearl diving and related industries were well known and recognized as important for Middle Eastern and Asian markets. So Aramco management assigned an appropriate engineering and scientific staff to examine pollution and contamination risks both onshore and offshore.

In Gulf waters, this entailed carefully inspecting all subsea life in the area, including coral reefs and oyster beds, and recording current conditions very precisely, so that any subsequent damage could be quickly noted in time to take corrective action. All sea life found off Saudi Arabia's Gulf coast was identified and catalogued.

Aramco thereby established a baseline of conditions for area marine life, and in 1977 the company published a book entitled *Biotopes of the Western Arabian Gulf* which could be used to guide future environmental protection efforts.

The Saudi Government also made use of this information and approach in surveying the Red Sea off the west coast, with its very large coral reefs, potentially vulnerable to sea traffic heading to and from the Suez Canal.

In August 1990, Saddam Hussein's Iraqi army invaded Kuwait. A coalition of countries, including the United States and Saudi Arabia, was formed to counter the invasion, and by January 1991 coalition forces were launching air attacks against the Iraqi forces. Iraq responded by crippling Kuwaiti oil production. Some 600 Kuwaiti oil wells were set ablaze. Most of the wells were destroyed either by the fires or by drastic extinguishing techniques employed by more than 20 expert wildfire and blowout control companies from all over the world. The damaged wells leaked large amounts of oil into pools onshore and into the Arabian Gulf. But an even greater environmental catastrophe lay ahead. The Iraqis opened the valves at the Sea Island oil terminal near Kuwait City, dumping millions of barrels of crude oil into the Gulf. The resulting oil slick covered an area of roughly 4,000 square miles. A long stretch of Saudi Arabia's northern Gulf coastline was "heavily impacted" by the oil spill, according to experts from Aramco's Environmental Engineering Division.

According to *The New York Times*, a 1993 study funded by UNESCO, the Gulf countries and the United States estimated that about half of the Kuwait oil spill eventually evaporated in the hot sun. About one million further barrels of oil were recovered from the sea, mostly by a large Saudi Aramco effort that employed booms and skimmers to capture the oil. An estimated two to three million barrels washed ashore, mainly in Saudi Arabia. "I was prepared in my mind for something large, but not for an oil spill of anything like that size," Abdulla Zaindin, Saudi Aramco's global oil spill coordinator, observed at the time.[1]

Saudi Aramco's spill recovery efforts in 1991 focused primarily on keeping the spreading oil away from the seawater intakes of the company's two northernmost Gulf installations – the oil desalting plant at Safaniya, just south of Kuwait, that

---

[1] "The Coast Recovers: Five Years After the Gulf Oil Spill," *Saudi Aramco Dimensions*, Fall 1996.

served the world's largest offshore field, and the reverse-osmosis water desalination plant at Tanajib, which supplied 1.5 million liters of water per day to allied military forces in the area and to the Saudi Aramco workforce.

In the week following the spill, company teams deployed more than 7 miles (11 kilometers) of protective booms in the waters around the seawater intake channels. When rough weather hit, oil began to find its way past the booms. Eventually sand banks were constructed to protect the saltwater intakes, and these proved to be effective.

By March the heavy concentration of oil had slipped south. By a fluke of nature, Manifa Bay and a large shallow bay in the south were positioned to catch the oil as it drifted southward. Manifa Bay became a major oil spill recovery site. It was awash with oil throughout the crisis and its outermost reaches were used as oil recovery sites by both Saudi Aramco and the Kingdom's Meteorology and Environmental Protection Administration (MEPA). Saudi Aramco provided technical and logistical support to other response teams under the Saudi Government's oversight.

Skimmer vessels recovered much oil in the open Gulf before it could reach the shoreline. Where the oil did reach the beaches, hundreds of company volunteers helped rescue and clean seabirds, sea turtles and other animals trapped in the oil.

The coastline in this area includes nine small bays and features salt marshes, intertidal mud flats, muddy sand beaches and rocky shorelines. The area is remote and sparsely populated, aside from Saudi Aramco facilities and two small fishing villages.

In the years following the Gulf oil spill, sites up and down the coast were studied by Saudi Aramco marine scientists as well as by outside specialists. They examined both "high-energy" areas like open beaches, coral reefs and other zones regularly affected by wave, sand or tidal action, and "low-energy" habitats like mudflats and salt marshes, where there is little movement to spur the natural breakdown of petroleum. The general conclusion of scientists five years after the spill was that high-energy habitats were returning – or in some cases had already returned – to normal, while low-energy zones were slower to heal.

Saudi Aramco specialists conducted long-term monitoring studies on the bioaccumulation of hydrocarbons and heavy metals along the Saudi coast. They found that on balance the elevated levels of aromatic hydrocarbons did not persist for more than a couple of years after the Kuwait oil spill.

Company scientists also studied the recovery of the coast's intertidal zone, the area between low and high tides. They were very surprised to find that there had been tremendous natural cleansing over most of the habitats along that shoreline.

The scientists recommended that further cleanup not be undertaken in most areas. They felt that the fragile ecosystem of the salt marshes and the intertidal habitats would suffer more damage from mechanical cleanup efforts than if left to the forces of nature, such as tides, waves, winds and biological and chemical breakdown. Of course, we should keep in mind that the area's hot climate and the high temperatures of Gulf seawater played a significant role in these natural actions.

The huge offshore Manifa field expansion was underway in 2013 with completion scheduled for late 2014. Saudi Aramco was determined to protect and preserve the aquatic zones endangered by the oil spill of 1991. By 2010, new drilling platforms were connected by environmentally sensitive causeways that allowed traditional water flows to continue and sea life to remain largely undisturbed.

Later studies by universities in Europe, the United States and Australia showed that damage to coral reefs, oyster beds and biotopes in general along the Saudi coast was relatively minor within two to three years after the spill, when compared with the baseline studies undertaken by Aramco in the 1970s.

My goal in discussing these various environmental episodes has been to show that the company, the Saudi Government and the Saudi public were exposed early on to potentially serious environmental problems and the need for effective solutions – as well as the need for public awareness and discussion of these vital issues. I have been pleased to see that the Saudi Government's policies and actions in this regard are advancing steadily to keep pace with the most advanced global environmental practices, consistent with the needs of a growing nation and an advanced and sophisticated energy industry.

Chapter 25
75th Anniversary

In 2008, Saudi Aramco unrolled a year-long celebration of the company's 75th anniversary – marking three-quarters of a century since the signing of the Concession Agreement that launched the Kingdom's oil industry. Twenty years had passed since the creation of the 100 percent Saudi-owned version of the company – Saudi Aramco. But internal focus groups, surveys and interviews with employees told the event organizers that virtually all members of the Aramco family – Saudis and expatriates alike – wanted to celebrate the full, expansive sweep of the company's development, from its American-inspired origins through its decades of relentless growth, side-by-side with the Kingdom in the march toward national development and all the way to the respected global energy enterprise it had become by the first decade of the 21st century. Saudi and expatriate employees alike also wanted to call attention to the vision of Saudi Arabia's modern founder, King Abdulaziz Al

Saud, who had actively encouraged the achievements of Aramco and created an environment in which it could flourish.

The anniversary year featured a number of celebrations, including a day of activities in Dhahran highlighted by the presence and participation of Saudi Arabia's current ruler – and son of Abdulaziz – King Abdullah. It was a perfect opportunity for the company's management and employees to look back over the decades of

King Abdullah ibn Abdulaziz in 2010.

accomplishments and advances, and at the same time generate an atmosphere of enthusiasm and anticipation for the exciting future that lay ahead.

King Abdullah traveled to Dhahran on May 20. He attended two major events that day. The first was the formal anniversary celebration, which included a tour of a special exhibition on the history of the Kingdom's oil enterprise. The King, accompanied by a number of Gulf leaders, was briefed on the exhibition by Saudi Aramco's president and CEO, Abdallah Jum'ah, who explained the significance of the displays. The King delivered an address to the invited guests, in which he thanked Saudi Aramco for its role in the nation's development. "I take this opportunity to thank Aramco and its present and previous employees," he said.

On an interactive message board at the exhibition, the King wrote this message in Arabic: "Thanks to God, who blessed us with his generous gifts, as we celebrate the occasion of the 75th Anniversary of the establishment of Saudi Aramco. We are proud of its achievements and its employees over all generations. You have always been an example of giving, sincerity and efficiency in work and in serving the country. I wish you God's help to continue this excellence for the good of the country and the world."

Petroleum Minister Ali Al-Naimi also delivered a compelling speech that focused on Aramco's role in the growth of the Kingdom and its people.

The exhibition and presentation took place in a huge air-conditioned tent, constructed of a very heavy plastic material, large and high enough to accommodate 3,000 people. The tent was divided into a huge auditorium with a stage and various display areas with high walls onto which pictures were projected, portraying the history of the company's major facilities and its steady course of expansion, both in difficult desert terrain and offshore in the Gulf. The images included highlights of employee training and development, and the accomplishments of Aramcons over the years.

Many retirees and current employees were present, and I thoroughly enjoyed renewing my acquaintance with many of the Saudis who had been a large part of my successful times with Aramco.

The King also laid the foundation for the King Abdulaziz Center for World Culture, to be constructed close to the first oil well, Dammam No. 7. The Cultural Center, to be completed in about 2014, was the company's gift to the country on the occasion of the 75th Anniversary. When open, the Center will include art and natural history museums, a public library (both print and digital), exhibition halls, theaters, restaurants, learning and creativity centers for children, youth and adults, a volunteerism center and other facilities. The Cultural Center is envisioned as a catalyst for cultural and social progress. It will introduce various national audiences to the wide range of cultures around the world and at the same time spotlight for visitors and Saudis alike the rich, diverse and evolving cultures of the Arabian Peninsula. The center will be housed in a new complex now under construction, an iconic architectural wonder designed by a world-class firm and inspired by the geology that brought about the Kingdom's oil miracle.

The Cultural Center project was the vision of Abdallah Jum'ah, who understood the importance of a well-prepared next generation in shaping the future not only of Saudi Aramco but also of the Kingdom itself.

Abdallah had invited me to attend the celebration, and I was delighted to fly to Dhahran for this historic event. I was told to contact Aramco Services Company (ASC) in Houston, which would arrange transportation for my wife Julie and me to Saudi Arabia, along with accommodations in Aramco visitors' quarters while there. When making our arrangements for the trip with ASC, I learned that Houston staff members were busily trying to locate the now-grown children of Aramco parents who had lived in Saudi Arabia in the early days – specifically, children who had met King Abdulaziz during his second visit to the company in January 1947. ASC had been tasked with inviting the "Kids of '47" to be part of the celebration in Dhahran. President Jum'ah, in setting the agenda of the anniversary program, had put forth the idea of contacting the "children" who had greeted the then King in 1947 and inviting

them to return to Dhahran and meet the current King on the night of the celebration – in a kind of reprise of the welcome they had given his father some six decades earlier.

A little background. The founder of Saudi Arabia, King Abdulaziz, made two trips to Aramco facilities during his reign. The first visit, on May 1, 1939, was to turn the valve to begin the loading of the first oil tanker at the Aramco port of Ras Tanura. During his second visit – to see and personally experience the growth of the company – King Abdulaziz demonstrated his support for expatriate Aramco families with a special reception for women and children in Dhahran on January 25, 1947. Although Saudi custom limited mixed-gender gatherings, this get-together was a notable exception. King Abdulaziz wanted to show his gratitude to the expatriate community by shaking the hand of every woman and child who approached him. He certainly made a great impression on Saudi and foreign employees as well.

Saudi Aramco celebrates its 75th Anniversary in the presence of King Abdullah ibn Abdulaziz.

"The King was a wonderful man," recalled Mrs. R.K. (Carol) Haug, one of the American mothers who attended the reception. "I remember to this day the big wonderful smile and a great feeling of warmth and protection from this man who I had been told was a great warrior."[1]

ASC had located 29 of the "children" who had met King Abdulaziz, all of whom who were able to attend the 75th anniversary ceremony with their spouses or close friends. Two of these were the twin daughters of Carol Haug, Jackie and Joyce, who eventually married Aramco employees, George Larsen and John Kriesmer, respectively.

Abdulaziz's son, King Abdullah, was most gracious and cordial at their meeting in Dhahran in 2008. A special tent and seating had been set up in the very same baseball and tennis court area where the original meeting with his father had taken place 61 years before. Attendees agree that the King was genuinely moved by this tribute to his father. King Abdullah viewed a retrospective portrayal of that memorable event of 1947, including photographic murals of the American children meeting his father and a visual tableau of today's Saudi Aramco youngsters dressed up in 1940s costumes to resemble the "Kids of '47" as they would have appeared to King Abdulaziz some six decades earlier.

The King warmly greeted the special guests of the moment – the actual "Kids of '47," long since grown, with families and grandchildren of their own. He also had an opportunity to greet the families of today's Aramco employees – spouses and children not just of Americans but of scores of other nationalities from around the world and, of course, many Saudis.

It was not surprising that King Abdullah personally relished the evening. He was delighted to receive his special guests, not only because his father had met and greeted them and their families in 1947, but also because he viewed these guests personally and symbolically as pioneering Aramcons who had been part of the history and advancement of his country.

In April 2002, then-Crown Prince Abdullah experienced a somewhat similar encounter in Texas. Ali Al-Naimi, Minister of Petroleum and Saudi Aramco Chairman, and Abdallah Jum'ah, company president and CEO, were expected at that time in Houston for a Saudi Aramco Board of Directors meeting, which was to

---

[1] McMurray, *Energy to the World: The Story of Saudi Aramco*, Vol. 1, p. 161.

be followed by the usual Board banquet with high-level management in attendance. Julie and I were invited to that banquet.

Two days before the meeting, we were advised by ASC that the banquet would be delayed slightly because Crown Prince Abdullah wanted to attend. The Crown Prince, acting on behalf of the seriously ailing King Fahd, was on an official visit to the United States at the time and was scheduled to meet with President George W. Bush at his ranch in Crawford, Texas, near the city of Waco. The King was not sure that the meeting with the U.S. President, scheduled for the same day as the Saudi Aramco banquet, would end in time for him to attend the dinner in Houston, so he asked that the banquet be rescheduled. The company set the banquet for two days later, on Saturday, April 27, 2002, and renamed the event "A Reception for Crown Prince Abdullah."

Some weeks ahead, Mary Norton, a former employee in Saudi Arabia and wife of Aramco annuitant Howard Norton, heard about the Crown Prince's visit to Texas. The Nortons received approval from the Saudi Embassy in Washington, D.C., to organize a special welcome for the Saudi leader. A group of Aramco retirees from the Austin area, who had spend decades with the company in Saudi Arabia, would be allowed to meet the Crown Prince on the tarmac of the Waco airport as he returned by bus from his meeting with President Bush at the Crawford ranch.

The meeting with the President lasted a few hours longer than anticipated, but the 35 retirees waited patiently near the royal airplane for the Crown Prince's arrival. The oldest retiree present was 106-year-old Eula Matthews, who was equipped with a bouquet of flowers and placed first in line to greet the Crown Prince. Mary Norton recalls standing next to her when the special black-and-gold bus pulled up at the plane. The door opened and Crown Prince Abdullah stepped out. Then, as Mary relates it, the Saudi leader showed an unexpected expression of surprise and delight that excited and relaxed the whole group. Smiling broadly, he took Eula's hand as Mary provided tidbits of Eula's background and that of her deceased husband, Dr. Charles Matthews. The couple had lived in Dhahran from 1948 to 1961. Eula also spoke a few words and presented the bouquet to the Crown Prince. And so it went, with each retiree meeting him and saying a few words, and with the Crown Prince replying in a relaxed and engaging fashion. To one woman wearing a necklace bearing her name in Arabic script, he said: "I like your necklace, Marion."

Two of the Crown Prince's nephews, Foreign Minister Prince Saud Al Faisal and

Saudi Ambassador to the U.S. Prince Bandar ibn Sultan, also mingled with the group. As the meeting drew to a close, the retirees were invited to the banquet in Houston, and were told that those who wanted to come would be picked up by the Petroleum Minister's airplane and flown to Houston on Saturday morning.

The Minister's plane brought a full load of retirees to the banquet, where the total guest count rose to about 400 people. ASC had scrambled to accommodate the extra guests, and the event proceeded seamlessly. Everyone milled about happily at the banquet reception and talked of old times. Julie and I were honored to be seated at a long elevated head table facing the guests, in the company of the Crown Prince and two of his sons; Ali Al-Naimi and Abdallah Jum'ah, as hosts; Prince Saud Al Faisal and Prince Bandar ibn Sultan; and the Mayor of Houston.

The Chairman, Minister Al-Naimi, made a very noteworthy speech, in which he highlighted the company's historic role in Saudi Arabia's development and pointed to the close ties that linked not only the U.S. and the Kingdom, but also the Saudi petroleum industry and its American counterparts, particularly in Texas. All in all, it was a delightful event that generated a considerable amount of goodwill.

No doubt King Abdullah recalled this remarkable encounter with expatriate retirees as he met six years later with the "Kids of '47" and today's Saudi Aramco community.

In reflecting on the 75th anniversary celebrations, I am struck by the fact that today's Aramcons not only honored the dazzling accomplishments of the past, but also set the stage for an even greater future. I was greatly impressed by the talented young Saudis I met during this trip – dynamic, intelligent, flexible young people, both men and women, who had absorbed the Aramco ethic and were confident they could overcome whatever challenges the future brought them. These employees were excited about participating in the next stage of the company's growth – because they understood it was a crucial part of the Kingdom's national development and would impact the entire country. They knew that Saudi Aramco and the Kingdom of Saudi Arabia would continue to grow up together, for the long-term benefit of the enterprise and the nation.

Chapter 26
Conclusion

Since my time at Aramco, the company now known as Saudi Aramco has grown in virtually every dimension – exhibiting impressive growth almost entirely under Saudi management. That Saudi management consists of personnel steeped in Aramco's corporate culture, most of them having advanced through the company organization and its extensive training and development systems, with young, trained Saudi-nationality Aramcons replacing retiring American Aramcons in an orderly and systematic manner.

The King and the Government have complete confidence in the company's management and have wisely refrained from installing bureaucrats in its organization. This is in sharp contrast to what has occurred to the petroleum industry in countries that went down the route of nationalization. In 1988, the Saudi Government and the four Aramco shareholder companies implemented the final provisions of the participation agreements, by which the government became the 100 percent owner of the renamed Saudi Aramco. The company then needed to market its own resources worldwide, while maintaining the former Aramco owners as preferred customers.

The company's first Saudi president and CEO, Ali Al-Naimi, was subsequently appointed Saudi Arabia's Minister of Petroleum as well as the company's Chairman

Ali Al-Naimi, first Saudi President and CEO of Aramco/Saudi Aramco and subsequently Minister of Petroleum and Mineral Resources, is shown below as a freshman at the American University in Beirut in 1957 (photo by Khalil Nasr) and opposite as Minister in 2004.

of the Board – establishing an unprecedented direct communication channel into the Government. Al-Naimi, who joined the company as a teenager, was a Bedouin youth and a natural leader who advanced through the entire organization, working in a wide variety of positions. He earned a Master's Degree in Geology from Stanford University and advanced through the same extraordinary Aramco development program that propelled many other Saudis into high-level positions. He had for some time advocated that the company advance into the downstream part of the business rather than remain primarily an oil- and gas-producing company, and thus he championed the merger of the Kingdom's domestic refining and marketing businesses into the fully-owned Saudi Aramco. These plants were – and are – based in Saudi Arabia, and some of them are partnerships with foreign corporations.

As Saudi Aramco's refining and marketing operations expanded worldwide, oil consumption continued to increase and prices to rise. Thus the company's oil exploration efforts expanded to include areas that were more expensive to develop and which in some cases were located outside the area delineated in the original Concession Agreement.

Three-dimensional seismic techniques, directional drilling and state-of-the-art production facilities were required. The company thus needed a larger research effort to develop and utilize all known production technologies. The 1980s were crucial years, therefore, as the company developed a central Exploration and Petroleum Engineering Center (EXPEC) in Dhahran to consolidate work that had previously been performed in the United States or Europe, or by shareholder companies.

EXPEC and its research facilities are now recognized by the entire oil industry as being unique and of outstanding capability. EXPEC now features an Advanced Research Center (EXPEC ARC), whose goal is to drive subsurface upstream research, creating innovative, high-impact solutions and tools that anticipate future exploration and production needs. EXPEC and EXPEC ARC are staffed with a healthy percentage of Saudi engineers and scientists, most of them educated at top-tier universities and institutions worldwide. The thrust of company expansions such as those mentioned above are directed toward expanding technical jobs and growing the overall Saudi economy, and all involve efforts to advance the education and training of young Saudis. To support these efforts in the E&P sector, the company now operates an Upstream Professional Development Center, whose aim is to provide the necessary training and work environment to produce the next generation of engineers and geoscientists ready to take on the challenges of future energy.

In 1984, Aramco made its first foray into the shipping business by purchasing four oil tankers. In time, the company's shipping subsidiary, Vela International Marine, was operating a fleet of very large crude carriers (VLCC's) in international trade, along with a numbers of smaller tankers operating in the Red Sea and Arabian Gulf. Today Vela, based in Dubai in the United Arab Emirates, is led and managed by Saudi professionals.

During this period, and until Ali Al-Naimi became Petroleum Minister and Chairman of Aramco, Abdallah Jum'ah, the son of a pearl diver, who advanced to become a senior executive, teamed with company president Al-Naimi. Together they pursued a long-range goal of expanding the company's scope internationally, to include a wide variety of downstream operations. These included refining and marketing operations in Asia – including China, Japan and South Korea – and in Texas in the United States, where the large refining and retail marketing company, Motiva Enterprises, is owned in partnership with Shell. Motiva, incidentally, operates a huge plant complex in Port Arthur, Texas, which was expanded in recent years to become the largest oil refinery in the United States.

Abdallah Jum'ah became president and CEO of Saudi Aramco in 1995, equipped with an outstanding – mostly non-technical – education, wide-ranging corporate experience and a deep interest in the training and education of employees. As CEO,

Abdallah S. Jum'ah, President and CEO of Saudi Aramco, in 2005.

he promoted a policy of continuing education for all employees, offering them every opportunity to grow their careers. Under his leadership, the company offered a unique communication and library access program that supplemented formal higher education. This process proved to be very popular among employees and achieved the results it sought. As president, he oversaw the biggest facilities expansion program in company history, involving the huge projects in the Empty Quarter and offshore in the Arabian Gulf, as well as large natural gas and crude oil facilities onshore.

In recent years, the Saudi Government and other governments in the Arabian Peninsula have become more and more concerned with providing for the future needs of their rapidly-expanding populations. All children in Saudi Arabia's fast-growing families have long been given the opportunity to attend out-of-Kingdom colleges and universities. The Government pays for higher education for both girls and boys seeking degrees at a large selection of universities inside or outside the Kingdom. The United States and Britain are probably the most popular countries selected for out-of-country studies. Most students from the Gulf countries have opted for degrees in the liberal arts rather than in the sciences and technology. This large influx of liberal arts graduates is greater than the number of available jobs, leading to increased unemployment, which could prove to be a potential source of unrest in many countries in the peninsula. Saudi Arabia was fortunate in that the College of Petroleum and Minerals was opened in Dhahran, next door to Aramco, in 1963, with its primary curriculum being engineering and mineral sciences. Then-Minister of Petroleum Yamani was the primary proponent of the college, which was approved by Royal Decree of King Faisal and installed under the Ministry of Petroleum. Its initial faculty was provided under a contractual agreement with nine highly-rated engineering and mineral science universities in the U.S., which in the early years provided rotating faculty and overall supervision. This college, later upgraded to a university, was accredited internationally. The university, along with family housing for the faculty, was built just outside Aramco's main residential community in Dhahran. Yamani asked for and obtained an initial contribution from Aramco of $11 million to move the project forward, so that the company could in time become a major employer of graduates.

This indeed became the case over time, as the college was transformed into the University of Petroleum and Minerals in 1975 and was renamed the King Fahd University of Petroleum and Minerals (KFUPM) in 1986. Many Aramco employees are KFUPM graduates, including Khalid Al-Falih, who became president and CEO of Saudi Aramco in 2009 after Abdallah Jum'ah's retirement. KFUPM today has 10,000 students and, along with other institutions in the Kingdom, has fulfilled the mission of teaching science and technology to Saudi undergraduates and graduates.

King Fahd University of Petroleum and Minerals in Dhahran, dominated by its futuristic tower, is seen here at twilight, adjacent to Saudi Aramco headquarters.

But these universities could not totally solve the problem of too many liberal arts graduates chasing too few jobs in the Kingdom.

Concern about Saudi college graduates needing jobs was a major motivation behind King Abdullah's decision to create the King Abdullah University of Science and Technology (KAUST) on the Red Sea coast north of Jeddah. He wanted capable college graduates with non-technical degrees to broaden their education by pursuing scientific studies and obtaining advanced degrees. Graduates of KAUST would help meet the Kingdom's need for trained personnel to man the expansion into not just basic oil and petrochemicals but also the entire range of derivatives and product production. Two huge world-class petrochemical complexes are already being built in Saudi Arabia, in partnership with Sumitomo Chemicals (Petro Rabigh II) and Dow Chemical (Sadara Chemical), with as many as three more projects in the planning stage. Also being considered are entries into the aluminum and fertilizer industries, to make use of the country's very large deposits of bauxite and potash, which fall under the responsibility of Petroleum Minister Al-Naimi.

In July 2006, Saudi Aramco was asked to build KAUST from scratch. The plan was to develop it on a large plot of land near the fishing village of Thuwal. At the groundbreaking ceremony in October 2007, the King declared: "We are living in an era of scientific and technological advancement. There is no real power without achieving progress in science and technology."

Saudi Aramco led the planning and supervised the construction of the multi-billion dollar project, which included a large campus with research facilities and a complete "city" to house and accommodate graduate students, faculty and their families. Also included in the funding were scholarships and endowments.

The KAUST campus opened as scheduled for classes in September 2009 – yes, in just over two years! Fifteen months later, in December 2010, at the first graduation ceremony, 292 Master's degrees were awarded. About one-third of these graduates intended to continue their studies in pursuit of doctoral degrees from this fully-accredited university.

In my view, the important lesson to be drawn from this and other projects like the King Abdulaziz Center for World Culture in Dhahran and the large public sports complex now being built by Saudi Aramco near Jeddah, is that the pattern of mutual cooperation between the Kingdom and Saudi Aramco continues unabated. King Abdullah continues to rely on the company as one of the Kingdom's prime

Khalid A. Al-Falih, President and CEO of Saudi Aramco. in 2011.

developmental partners – he once remarked to Minister Al-Naimi that he knew Aramco, when implementing these projects, would not misuse "a single *halalah*" [less than a penny].

The company's current president and CEO, Khalid Al-Falih, is the son of one of Aramco's first Saudi vice presidents, Abdul Aziz Al-Falih, now retired, who was in charge of the Materials Supply Organization. Khalid is an engineering graduate of Texas A&M University with a Master's degree from the KFUPM.[1]

---

[1] In 2010, Texas A&M honored Khalid Al-Falih with its Outstanding International Alumnus Award.

From the story we have told, it can be seen that Aramco and the Saudi Government have advanced virtually in parallel over the years – as the oil industry has developed, so has the Government's response to the people and their aspirations. This is a history of mutual progress over more than 75 years, with each partner relying on and supporting the other.

Meanwhile, what has happened to the Aramcons who participated in this partnership over the years? Retired Aramcons and other former employees have remained remarkably close. Their unique experience at the heart of Saudi Arabia's development story has created bonds that cannot be broken. American Aramcons continue to hold large reunions throughout the United States every two years, always at major resorts, alternating between the East and West Coasts and in Texas and its surrounds. Participants at these gatherings can number 1,500 to 2,000, including families and some Saudi retirees. Reunions are also organized in Europe by Dutch ex-employees, most of whom worked in the company's offices in the Netherlands. Get-togethers are regularly held in other countries as well, such as Pakistan, and even, rather amazingly, in the tiny state of Goa, once a Portuguese colony and now part of India. In the early days at Aramco, American employees often hired Goanese domestic help, and I once visited my old housekeeper, Francis Pereira, at his home in Goa a few days after a reunion of Goanese Aramco housekeepers and company employees had taken place in a nearby village. They reminisced excitedly about the "good old days." (South Asian housekeepers earned substantial amounts, by their nations' standards, during their work at Aramco, and many were able to build houses and create businesses back home with their savings from these jobs.)

Many Americans have attended reunions back in Saudi Arabia, which have been organized by Saudi retirees, usually coordinated by Ali Baluchi, former general manager of Community Services, who secures company sponsorship and help where necessary. These reunions feature dinners and parties, of course, but also frequently include trips to distant parts of Saudi Arabia and visits to ancient historical and archaeological sites.

There have been, of course, many children born to the thousands of retired American Aramcons. Most of these children were born in Saudi Arabia, often at the Aramco hospital in Dhahran, and they frequently have a special affection for the land of their birth. They now hold reunions in the United States, where they have dubbed themselves "Aramco Brats." It is not surprising that my own sons were born in Saudi Arabia. One of them, Gary, married an American girl who was also born in the Kingdom. Their first child, my grandson, was also born in Saudi Arabia, where Gary worked for a few years as an engineer.

Many of the sons and daughters of Aramcons of Saudi nationality have gone on to work for the company and they, too, feel a close connection not only with Saudi Aramco but also with each other. The bicultural relationship of the Aramcon becomes more apparent when looking at the current Saudi Aramco management, which is virtually entirely Saudi. Almost all of the company's senior management executives are Saudis who have risen through the ranks – through corporate training, development and work assignments – and a number of them, too, like Al-Falih, are second- and third-generation Aramcons.

Throughout all this, the Saudis have developed a solid, dynamic corporate culture, incorporating the no-nonsense, achievement-oriented standards and processes of the Aramco Legacy and the collaborative and innovative features of Saudi society. The result is a business culture that is second to none. The Saudis of Saudi Aramco are comfortable in all societies, and they mingle easily with Westerners and Easterners in their work or travels. Whether at home or abroad, they solidly exemplify their Arab values, dress and language, and Islamic religious orientation. So now, with Saudi Aramco staffed top-to-bottom mostly with Saudi Arabs, the Aramco corporate culture has become a distinctive and indeed unique national legacy that continues on as a solid, well-functioning part of Saudi society.

Saudi Arabia is on the brink of a new era, and the Aramco Legacy is playing a key role in guiding the Kingdom toward that future. Unlike many developing countries that seem to have no clear vision of their economic future, Saudi Arabia is pursuing a carefully-developed plan to create new industries and jobs to accommodate substantial population growth and provide a prosperous life for future generations. King Abdullah, with his plans for a network of Economic Cities, vigorous free enterprise, a national "knowledge economy" and the like, is moving the country toward a new global role that makes the most effective use of Saudi resources, nurtures the growth of the global economy and provides for the needs of the Saudi population.

Saudi Aramco is participating in this process in many ways. It is moving the Kingdom toward national energy conservation and efficiency, to maximize use of precious hydrocarbon resources; it is building a globally-oriented industrial engine based on plastics and other downstream products that will create new companies, jobs and enterprise opportunities; and it is encouraging innovation, creativity, technological progress, instantaneous communications and other aspects of the "knowledge economy."

To position the company for the new era, Saudi Aramco has launched an Accelerated Transformation Program (ATP), which will prepare employees for the dramatic changes that lie ahead. Khalid Al-Falih unveiled this ambitious program at a management seminar in the summer of 2011, describing it as an initiative to "unlock the company's full human potential."

Al-Falih explicitly linked the initiative with the achievements of the "old Aramco." He called attention to "our long-standing friendship with the United States" and paid tribute to "the American pioneers who helped provide the firm foundation upon which today's Saudi Aramco has been built."

To outsiders, the visible results of the planned transformation are likely to be the changing nature of the company's business portfolio and its expanded operational profile, as it moves from being a traditional oil and gas company to a fully-integrated global energy and chemicals enterprise. But many of the most significant changes in the transformation will be intangible, and will have more to do with people than with plants or pipelines.

The changing demographics of the workforce are helping to drive the transformation and provide the company with a great opportunity for meaningful change. "Saudi Arabia has a large youth population," Al-Falih said, "and at Saudi Aramco, we have a significant number of employees who will be retiring during the next decade. As a result, in five years' time, nearly 40 percent of our workforce will be under the age of 30. These 'Generation Y' employees have never known life without computers, are immersed in instant communications and social media, thrive on multitasking, and have been so influenced by technology and globalization that their work styles, lifestyles, values and expectations differ markedly from those of previous generations."

Preparing young Saudis to take on the challenges of a bold new future – that is the essence of what is required today and, despite the differences in generations, this echoes our efforts in Aramco's early days to create a Saudi workforce that was up to the challenge of running a world-class petroleum company. The young Saudis from that era are Saudi Aramco's leaders today, and they clearly met the challenge.

When I visit Saudi Aramco these days, I see the new company flourishing and at the same time maintaining the corporate culture that made Aramco great. I feel pride in our achievements, but also great humility at the privilege of witnessing the company's rise to heights we could never have imagined. Indeed, Aramco and Saudi Arabia grew up together – but the process continues. In fact, it is only the beginning.

Frank and Julie Jungers at Shaybah, in the Rub' al-Khali, during a return visit in 2006.

Appendix 1
Chronology

1932 – Abdulaziz Al Saud unites Hejaz and Najd, creating the Kingdom of Saudi Arabia.

1933 – Standard Oil of California (Socal) secures a concession from the Saudi Government to explore for and produce petroleum in Saudi Arabia; establishes California Arabian Standard Oil Company (CASOC) to operate the concession.

1936 – The Texas Company (which became Texaco) acquires 50 percent of CASOC.

1938 – CASOC discovers first Saudi crude oil in commercial quantities.

1939 – First tanker-load of Saudi crude is exported from Ras Tanura.

1941 – The U.S. enters World War II. CASOC suspends most operations.

1944 – CASOC changes its name to Aramco and resumes operations as the war winds down.

1945 – Ras Tanura (RT) Refinery begins operations.

1946 – Jersey Standard Oil (or Esso, later Exxon and ExxonMobil) and Socony-Vacuum (later Mobil, later part of ExxonMobil) acquire shares of Aramco.

1947 – Frank Jungers joins Aramco, working at its San Francisco headquarters.

1947 – Jungers travels to Saudi Arabia, working as liaison to Bechtel Corporation in the RT Refinery Upgrade Project.

1948 – Jungers receives permanent assignment as a design and project engineer in RT for refinery and terminal shipping projects.

1952 – Jungers receives his first administrative assignment, supervising maintenance and shops crafts personnel in RT refinery and in the offloading terminal.

1953 – King Abdulaziz dies and is succeeded by his son, Crown Prince Saud. The new King's half-brother, Prince Faisal, is named Crown Prince.

1953–54 – Jungers visits oil companies in other producing countries as part of a committee studying best practices in good corporate citizenship.

1956 – Jungers is named general superintendent, Dhahran pipeline maintenance, shops, transportation, communications facilities and engineering.

1956 – Aramco confirms that Ghawar and Safaniya are the world's largest onshore and offshore oilfields respectively.

1959–61 – Jungers joins Aramco's "Think Committee", a policy sounding board, as a part-time assignment. He chairs the committee for six months.

1960 – The Organization of Petroleum Exporting Countries (OPEC) is formed. Saudi Arabia is a founding member.

1961 – Jungers serves on a special committee for Aramco's long-range planning needs.

1962–63 – Jungers studies Arabic and Arabian culture during a one-year assignment at the Middle East Center for Arabic Studies in Shemlan, Lebanon.

1963 – Jungers holds acting supervisory positions in the Abqaiq oil production district, including operations and drilling.

1964 – King Saud abdicates and is succeeded by Crown Prince Faisal.

1964–65 – Jungers is named assistant general manager of the New York office, handling liaison with shareholder companies' technical personnel. As chairman of shareholder directors' Study Group, he supervises the Manufacturing and Oil Supply Departments as well as the Financial Department in New York.

1965–66 – Jungers serves as supervisor of producing operations at Abqaiq.

1966–68 – Jungers is named member of the Policy and Planning staff for Arab Relations. He serves as deputy company representative in Riyadh. He works as director of the Planning and Economics Department and then serves as general manager of Government Relations.

1969 – Jungers is named senior vice president of Concession Affairs.

1970 – Jungers is appointed senior vice president of Finance and Relations. He attends the London oil company talks.

1971 – Jungers attends the Tehran oil-pricing negotiations. Later, he is named president of Aramco.

1973 – Jungers becomes chairman and CEO of Aramco.

1973 – Negotiations with the Saudi Government results in the acquisition of 25 percent of Aramco and preliminary pathway to onward purchase over the years.

1973 – Saudi Arabia leads – and Aramco implements – an oil embargo against the United States and other countries that supported Israel in the October War against Egypt and Syria. The price of crude oil quadruples.

1975 – The Master Gas System (MGS) project is launched, to gather and process the natural gas produced in association with crude oil.

1975 – King Faisal is shot and killed by a deranged nephew. Faisal's half-brother, Crown Prince Khalid, succeeds as King. Jungers pays respects to Royal Family in Riyadh.

1976 – At Aramco's recommendation, King Khalid issues a Royal Decree creating the Saudi Consolidated Electric Company (SCECO) in the Eastern Province.

1978 – Jungers retires from Aramco. Afterward, he serves as a consultant to Bechtel Corporation on oil industry acquisitions; companies acquired included Dual Drilling Co. and Welltech Co.

1980 – The Saudi Government acquires 100 percent participation interest in Aramco.

1983 – Ali I. Al-Naimi is named president of Aramco, the first Saudi to hold the position.

1988 – The Saudi Arabian Oil Company (Saudi Aramco) is established.

1993 – At the Government's request, Saudi Aramco takes over Saudi Arabia's domestic refining, marketing, distribution and joint venture refining interests.

1995 – Saudi Aramco president and CEO Ali I. Al-Naimi is named Minister of Petroleum and Mineral Resources of Saudi Arabia, and chairman of Saudi Aramco. Abdullah S. Jum'ah succeeds him as president and CEO of Saudi Aramco.

1998 - Saudi Aramco, Texaco and Shell establish Motiva Enterprises, a major refining and marketing joint venture in the southern and eastern United States.

2007 – Saudi Aramco, ExxonMobil, Sinopec and the Fujian Provincial Government form refining and marketing joint ventures in China.

2008 – Jungers attends Saudi Aramco's celebration of the 75th anniversary of the original Concession Agreement. King Abdullah visits Dhahran to take part.

2009 – Khalid A. Al-Falih is named president and CEO of Saudi Aramco, succeeding Abdallah S. Jum'ah.

Jungers has served on the following Boards of Directors over a period of 30 years:

Georgia-Pacific
Donaldson, Lufkin & Jenrette
Thermo Electron
Thermal Instrument Company
Hyster Corp
ESCO Corp
Star Technologies
Oregon Bank
Statia Terminals
Horizon Shipping Lines
Dual Drilling Company

Jungers has also served as a trustee of the following charitable and educational organizations:

American University of Cairo (AUC)
Oregon Health & Science University Foundation
University of Washington Foundation
U.S. National Council of World Wildlife Fund
Nature Conservancy of Oregon
Goodwill Industries International

Appendix 2
Company Leaders

Chief Executive Officers (CEOs)		Chairmen of Board of Directors	
Aramco		*Aramco*	
Harry D. Collier	1944–51	Harry D. Collier	1944–51
William S.S. Rodgers	1951–52	William S.S. Rodgers	1951–52
Fred A. Davies	1952–59	Fred A. Davies	1952–59
Norman "Cy" Hardy	1959–61	Norman "Cy" Hardy	1959–68
Thomas C. Barger	1961–69	Thomas C. Barger	1968–69
Robert I. Brougham	1969–70	Robert I. Brougham	1969–70
Liston F. Hills	1971–73	Liston F. Hills	1970–73
Frank Jungers	1973–78	Frank Jungers	1973–78
John J. Kelberer	1978–88	John J. Kelberer	1978–88
Saudi Aramco		*Saudi Aramco*	
Ali I. Al-Naimi	1988–95	Hisham M. Nazer	1988–95
Abdallah S. Jum'ah	1995–2008	Ali I. Al-Naimi	1995–
Khalid A. Al-Falih	2009–		

Index